Tarot

SIGNPOSTS ALONG THE PATH

A Spiritual Approach to the Tarot
by Laura E. Clarson

Copyright ©1995 by Laura E. Clarson

Published by Visionary Enterprises
5635 N. E. 12th Ave.
Portland, OR 97211, USA

ISBN 0-945766-12-2

All rights reserved including the right of
reproduction in whole or in part in any form.

Illustrations from the Cosmic Tarot deck
reproduced by permission of Norbert Lösche.

Copyright © 1988 by F. X. Schmid.

Further reproduction prohibited.

The Cosmic Tarot Deck by Norbert Lösche.

Cover design by Reneé Renfrow.

10 9 8 7 6 5 4 3 2 1

Printed in the United States of America.

Other books by Laura Clarson:

Tarot Unveiled: The Method to its Magic
Finding your Soul Chart Through Esoteric Astrology

The following videotapes by Laura Clarson
are available from Visionary Enterprises:

Beginning Tarot
The Minor Arcana
Intermediate Tarot
Advanced Tarot
The Astrology of Romance
Basic Handwriting Analysis
Basic Numerology
How to Read Playing Cards

Table of Contents

Introduction — 1
Structure of the Tarot — 1
Accessing the Unconscious with the Tarot — 2
Tarot as a Language — 3
Getting Started — 3
Choosing and Storing a Deck — 3
Getting Acquainted With a New Deck — 4
Phrasing the Question — 4
How to Prepare to Consult the Cards — 5
What is a Spread? — 5
How to Shuffle and Spread the Cards — 6
How to Personalize the Cards — 6
Creating a Tarot Journal — 6
Choosing Your Personal Cards — 7
Checking the Accuracy of Your Spreads — 7
Reading for Yourself — 7
Reading for Others — 8
The Best Approach for Reading Cards for Others — 8
What If You Are Expected to Predict? — 9
Tact in Your Delivery — 9
Focus on the Questioner — 10

The Major Arcana — 11
Many Major Arcana Cards In a Spread — 11
Meanings of the Major Arcana Cards — 12
0 THE FOOL (Innocence) — 15
I THE MAGICIAN (Innovation) — 16
II THE HIGH PRIESTESS (Psychic Powers) — 17
III THE EMPRESS (Fertility) — 18
IV THE EMPEROR (Order) — 19
V THE HIEROPHANT (Spiritual Ritual) — 20
VI THE LOVERS (Powerful Attraction) — 21
VII THE CHARIOT (Motivation) — 22
VIII JUSTICE (Balance) — 23
IX THE HERMIT (Guidance) — 24
X WHEEL OF FORTUNE (Changing Cycles) — 25
XI STRENGTH (Healing) — 26
XII THE HANGED MAN (Suspension) — 27
XIII DEATH (Transformation) — 28

XIV TEMPERANCE (Moderation)	29
XV THE DEVIL (Temptation)	30
XVI THE TOWER (Catalyst for Change)	31
XVII THE STAR (Sense of Purpose)	32
XVIII THE MOON (Hidden Forces)	33
XIX THE SUN (Joy)	34
XX JUDGMENT (Reward)	35
XXI THE WORLD (Synthesis)	36
THE UNKNOWABLE (Hidden Information)	37

The Minor Arcana 38

Swords 39
Cups 41
Wands 43
Pentacles 45
Aces Through Tens 47
Three or Four of a Kind in a Spread 48
Preponderance of Suits 48

Aces 49
THE ACE OF SWORDS (Courage) 50
THE ACE OF CUPS (New Friendships) 51
THE ACE OF WANDS (Creativity) 52
THE ACE OF PENTACLES (New Financial Venture) 53

Twos 54
THE TWO OF SWORDS (Stalemate) 55
THE TWO OF CUPS (Friendship) 56
THE TWO OF WANDS (Collaboration) 57
THE TWO OF PENTACLES (Balancing Financial Affairs) 58

Threes 59
THE THREE OF SWORDS (Heartbreak) 60
THE THREE OF CUPS (Celebration) 61
THE THREE OF WANDS (Creative Flow) 62
THE THREE OF PENTACLES (Mastery) 63

Fours 64
THE FOUR OF SWORDS (Recuperation) 65
THE FOUR OF CUPS (Apathy) 66
THE FOUR OF WANDS (Partnership) 67
THE FOUR OF PENTACLES (Security) 68

Fives 69
  THE FIVE OF SWORDS (Betrayal) 70
  THE FIVE OF CUPS (Regret) 71
  THE FIVE OF WANDS (Competition) 72
  THE FIVE OF PENTACLES (Insecurity) 73
Sixes 74
  THE SIX OF SWORDS (Assistance) 75
  THE SIX OF CUPS (The Past) 76
  THE SIX OF WANDS (Triumph) 77
  THE SIX OF PENTACLES (Financial Aid) 78
Sevens 79
  THE SEVEN OF SWORDS (Mistrust) 80
  THE SEVEN OF CUPS (Imagination) 81
  THE SEVEN OF WANDS (Position of Advantage) 82
  THE SEVEN OF PENTACLES (New Business Perspective) 83
Eights 84
  THE EIGHT OF SWORDS (Restriction) 85
  THE EIGHT OF CUPS (Withdrawal) 86
  THE EIGHT OF WANDS (Swiftness) 87
  THE EIGHT OF PENTACLES (Education) 88
Nines 89
  THE NINE OF SWORDS (Intense Anxiety) 90
  THE NINE OF CUPS (Wish Fulfillment) 91
  THE NINE OF WANDS (Watch and Wait) 92
  THE NINE OF PENTACLES (Comfortable Home) 93
Tens 94
  THE TEN OF SWORDS (Disaster) 95
  THE TEN OF CUPS (Love) 96
  THE TEN OF WANDS (Stress and Pressure) 97
  THE TEN OF PENTACLES (Material Prosperity) 98
The Court Cards 99
Princesses 101
  THE PRINCESS OF SWORDS (Forceful Communication) 102
  THE PRINCESS OF CUPS (Social Messages) 103
  THE PRINCESS OF WANDS (Enthusiasm) 104
  THE PRINCESS OF PENTACLES (Financial Dealings) 105
Princes 106
  THE PRINCE OF SWORDS (Assertive Action) 107
  THE PRINCE OF CUPS (Congeniality) 108
  THE PRINCE OF WANDS (Energy) 109
  THE PRINCE OF PENTACLES (Shrewd Business Skills) 110

Queens	111
THE QUEEN OF SWORDS (Strong-Willed)	112
THE QUEEN OF CUPS (Nurturing)	113
THE QUEEN OF WANDS (Exuberance)	114
THE QUEEN OF PENTACLES (Practicality)	115
Kings	116
THE KING OF SWORDS (Intelligence)	117
THE KING OF CUPS (Protective)	118
THE KING OF WANDS (Entrepreneur)	119
THE KING OF PENTACLES (Business Ability)	120

Combinations 121
Reading Spreads 127

The Purpose of Spreads	127
The Timing and Advice Cards	127
Timing	127
The Advice of the Cards	128
The Star of Insight Spread	128
Meanings of Positions in the Spread	128
The Crossroads Spread	132
Meanings of Positions in the Spread	132
Spreads Relating to Soul Purpose and Life Direction	135
The Soul Purpose Spread	135
Meanings of Positions in the Spread	136
The Life Reading Spread	138
Meanings of Positions in the Spread	139
The Life Reading Update	142

Introduction

Structure of the Tarot

We can only speculate about the origins of the Tarot symbols because research has failed to unearth conclusive evidence about its true beginnings. The symbols of the Major Arcana cards are believed to describe the process of initiation used in ancient Sumeria and Egypt. Fortunetelling gypsies brought the Tarot from the east to Europe where they were in general usage by the late 14th century. The Minor Arcana cards were added to the deck later as it was adapted as a card game. The validity of each Tarot symbol is not based upon historical tradition but rather upon the inherent power of each archetypal image.

The Tarot deck of 78 cards is structured into two groups:

- 22 Major Arcana cards
- 56 Minor Arcana cards

The **Major Arcana** begins with the Fool and ends with the World. Of the 22 Major Arcana cards, only the Fool in the form of the Joker remains in present day playing cards. The Major Arcana cards refer to the process of spiritual awakening through growth. They pertain more to psychological issues and spiritual lessons than to the ordinary affairs of life.

The **Minor Arcana** is similar to an ordinary deck of playing cards with four suits, each numbered from Ace to King. The Princess in the Tarot deck is called a Jack in the standard deck. The Tarot deck also includes four Princes that are missing from the present day deck of playing cards.

The four suits in the Tarot deck are Swords, Cups, Wands, and Pentacles. In a deck of playing cards, Swords correspond to Spades, Cups to Hearts, Wands to Clubs, and Pentacles to Diamonds. **Swords** pertain to mental pursuits, conflict, and struggle. **Cups** involve emotional situations and relationships. **Wands** express creativity, intuition, and enterprise. **Pentacles** relate to money and business affairs.

Upright cards (right side up) and **reversed** cards (upside down) are interpreted differently in Tarot card reading. The reversed meaning is not always opposite to the upright meaning but instead can show an exaggeration of the upright quality. For example, the 3 of Pentacles refers to mastery and discrimination when upright, but when reversed, its good qualities have been distorted into perfectionism and criticism.

Often, when a difficult card is reversed, the reversed meaning is encouraging because it show the problem is abating. For example, when upright, the 5 of Wands means disputes and strife, but when reversed, there is peace after conflict.

Reversed cards are represented in this book by the letter R following the card name, such as 3 of Pentacles R and Five of Wands R for the example cards above.

Accessing the Unconscious with the Tarot

When we learn a new language, we must learn the meanings of new words and string them together in sentences. The 78 cards plus their reversed meanings provide 156 different meanings that we use to describe the workings of the unconscious mind. By accessing the unconscious through the Tarot, active imagination, or our dreams, we can tap into both the personal and collective unconscious.

The **personal unconscious** contains every sensation, memory, thought, and emotion that we have experienced in this incarnation since conception. Through hypnotherapy, blocked memories and traumas have become accessible and often have explained and resolved phobias. The Tarot is accurate and effective as a tool for shedding light on the unconscious without the necessity for hypnosis or trance.

The **collective unconscious** is the common pool of human experience that we have shared with all of humanity from antiquity. The experience of motherhood is the same for us as it was for the cave dwellers because the mother archetype is universal for all humans. As a species, we are innately responsive to archetypes much as animals have inborn instincts. Carl Jung proved that someone completely unfamiliar with an archetype could have a vivid and meaningful dream about it. For example, an uneducated woman dreamed that a goddess wearing horns on her head was giving her a gift. She later discovered that the Egyptian goddess Hathor had always been pictured that way and was a nurturing mother figure in ancient Egyptian mythology.

The Tarot gives us access to our own unconscious awareness about the issues we question. As we concentrate on the question and shuffle, we stop shuffling when our inner intuitive self signals to us that the cards are in the order needed to accurately reflect our answers back to us. When we are truly centered as we shuffle the cards and humbly ask for insight about our question, we tap into the well of universal knowledge available to all of us and find our own answers.

Tarot as a Language

Since the pictures on the Tarot cards serve as our guide to the workings of the unconscious realms, it is important that they be specific and clearly defined. In the same way that the words "skillful" and "expert" are similar yet decidedly different in meaning, the 8 of Pentacles and the 3 of Pentacles each represent subtle differences in skill levels. By being precise in our meanings for each card, we can start with a clear sense of a card's meaning before trying to blend it with another. I have updated and modernized the meanings of many cards to accommodate our modern lifestyle which includes such things as the information highway, supersonic air travel, and subliminal self-help tapes. The 8 of Wands which traditionally related to swiftness and the arrows of love becomes air travel and on-line love "chats" today. I have tried to make each card relevant to our high tech, complex society without losing its essential traditional meaning.

Getting Started

Choosing and Storing a Deck

I recommend starting out with a deck with fairly traditional symbols and a different picture on each of the 78 cards. Look for a scene or picture rather than just five Wands or six Swords on the Minor Arcana cards so that you can associate the picture with the meaning of the card. Pick a deck that fascinates you and appeals to you aesthetically. Often, the first deck comes as a gift from a friend and only later is replaced by one that truly resonates.

This book is illustrated with the **Cosmic Tarot deck.** The images on these cards are both powerful and graceful, with special depth and charisma in the "face cards" of the Minor Arcana court cards. The portrait quality and elegance of the male and female characters help to get to know them as "real people." The romantic desert scenery and costumes combined with modern imagery create a sense of mystery in everyday life. Most of the images used in the Cosmic Tarot carry the spirit of traditional Tarot symbolism.

Other decks commonly used to begin learning Tarot are:

- The **Hanson-Roberts** deck
- The **Rider Waite** or **Albano-Waite** deck
- The **Aquarian** deck
- The **Morgan-Greer** deck

Your Tarot deck should be treated as a special ritual object when not in use and stored in a box, silk scarf, or bag. Allowing others to shuffle your deck is acceptable if you feel comfortable with it. Alternatives would be shuffling for others when you are reading for them or having a second deck only for your own personal use.

Getting Acquainted With a New Deck

To blend your energies with the new deck, try sleeping with it under your pillow or nearby, carrying the cards in a pocket or purse, randomly shuffling the cards periodically, and drawing one card a day for a period of a week. Look up the meaning of the card and when the meaning seems especially relevant to your life situation, you will know that the cards are ready for use.

Phrasing the Question

The person asking the question of the Tarot cards is called the questioner and in this book will be considered to be a female for the purpose of simplicity. When consulting the Tarot, it is best to avoid "yes" or "no" questions or questions that are confusing or ambiguous. Often, we ask questions made on assumptions rather than facts and become disillusioned or confused by the answers from the cards. For example, a question like: "Will I have enough money to move and to rent a house in Beaverton, Oregon?" could create more confusion than clarity. A positive or negative response to this question would still be confusing because you wouldn't know which part of the question was being referred to. There are really five separate issues here: money, moving, renting, a home, and Beaverton, Oregon. We cannot assume that any of these ideas are desirable without separating them and asking about the advisability of each one. A better way to ask about these issues would be: "Please give me insight and clarity about my money situation." After absorbing the response to that question, we could request insight and clarity about each of the other separate issues: moving, Beaverton, renting, and a house. By breaking down our question into separate issues, we are able to interpret the answers with more precision and detail. The process of allowing the Tarot to talk about our issues of concern rather than just answer questions opens our minds to hear what the cards are saying.

How to Prepare to Consult the Cards

It is best to take several deep breaths and get centered before shuffling the cards. A special prayer, mantrum, or invocation helps to establish a respectful attitude about consulting the cards. Many readers visualize connecting to their Higher Power and guides in the area a foot above the crown chakra at the top of the head. If you are reading for someone else, you might also include their Higher Power and guides as you get grounded and centered to ask their question.

An attitude of reverence and a humble desire for help and clarity allow the clearest connection to the wisdom of the Tarot. When the person shuffling is distracted or ungrounded, the cards often reflect the nervous energy around the person rather than providing deeper insight. Asking the same question in succession can create confusion since the first response holds the greatest clarity and power. If you do not understand what the cards are saying, it is better to leave the spread out and ask for intuitive insight about it over a day or two, rather than reshuffling and asking again.

It is also a good idea to write your spreads down when you first begin to read cards so that you can go back over them for validation. Many times, our early spreads have an especially magical quality characteristic of "beginner's luck" that welcomes us and encourages us to continue to explore the Tarot.

What is a Spread?

A spread is a layout of cards in a certain order in which each position has a particular meaning about your question. For example, the simplest spreads often have a position for past, present, and future of the issue in question. See the chapter on "Reading Spreads" for five spreads included in this book. It is necessary to have your spread in mind before you start shuffling so that the cards that fall in each position will be clear in answering your question.

How to Shuffle and Spread the Cards

To thoroughly mix the cards so that some will be upright and others reversed, shuffle a new deck 5-10 times or until you feel they are ready for use. Once you have initially mixed the direction of the cards in a new deck, they should be kept randomly mixed rather than restored to all one direction. Some readers shuffle the cards a set number of shuffles and cuts for each question. I found that I knew when to stop shuffling because the cards would feel stiff and hard to push back together when they were ready. Each person has an individual signal from the intuition to let her know the cards are ready to be spread for interpretation. It is not necessary to cut the cards unless you prefer that step. After the cards have been shuffled, hold them lengthwise in your hand and deal the cards by flipping them over sideways. Do not turn them over from top to bottom because that will change the upright and reversed directions of the cards.

How to Personalize the Cards

Get to know each card by looking at the pictures, reading the meaning, and thinking of specific events in your life that reflect the energy of the card. Allow the scene on the picture to conjure up a feeling in you that comes from the heart and solar plexus area. That feeling will bring images about personal experiences that tie in with the energy of that specific archetype. A strictly memorized, cerebral approach to the Tarot can seem mechanical and restrict access to the intuitive levels of interpretation. A good way to experience each card is to draw a card when you get up each day and focus on what it means for you for the rest of that day.

Creating a Tarot Journal

A special journal with a page devoted to each card is a way to organize your impressions about the cards as they develop. You might start out jotting down a few lines from books, movies, and personal experiences by free-associating about each card. Especially notice the feelings you experience during the course of the day, such as impatience or excitement, and decide which of the cards most describes it. By associating feelings and psychological traits with the cards, you will create a personal language using the cards that will allow you to describe the full range of human emotions, much as drama and literature do.

Focus first on the cards that attract or repel you. The ones that feel neutral or hard to comprehend will gradually come into focus if you don't force things. The Court cards include the Kings, Queens, Princes, and Princesses and are the face cards in the Tarot deck. A certain card may remind you of an important person you know and could be used to represent that person in your readings.

Choosing Your Personal Cards

After examining all the cards in the deck, choose one card from the Major Arcana cards to represent your inner spiritual self and a Minor Arcana card to reflect your outer personality. Let your intuition and feelings of attraction guide you in this choice. See the Soul Purpose Spread in the chapter on "Reading Spreads" for the Major Arcana card connected to your soul purpose.

Checking the Accuracy of Your Spreads

Usually, the Tarot is amazingly helpful and insightful in answering a question. At times, however, you or someone else may fail to maintain focus and concentration when shuffling and will create a jumbled and inaccurate spread. How can you know when this has occurred? Often, you will sense that the cards are not right when you have difficulty getting clearance to stop shuffling. After you spread out the cards, you can check the cards in the positions referring to the past and present to see if the cards there make sense with what is actually going on. If they do seem relevant, the cards relating to the future will most likely also hold true. If they don't ring true or only marginally fit the situation, it is best to re-shuffle after getting grounded and centered again.

Reading for Yourself

Your ability to stay objective and remove your personal wishes from the shuffling and reading will determine how well you can read for yourself. Many readers can read for themselves successfully when they are able to interpret the cards for themselves as impersonally as they read for others.

Much of this book and the five spreads included are designed to facilitate your inner exploration of the Tarot symbols for yourself. You will explore your destiny and purpose for being here from both the cosmic level of your life purpose and the immediate direction of your everyday life.

Reading for Others

Readings for close friends and family can also be tricky because your preconceived notions and wishes can interfere. It is often best to wait until you have developed some confidence about your ability to read cards before reading for certain family members or friends. Avoid those who may undermine your progress by implying that your accuracy is related to your previous knowledge of them rather than your competency.

The most validating way to learn Tarot is to read for those you know very little or nothing about and get their feedback about how the readings dovetail with their lives. Be sure to let those you read for in this context know that you are new to Tarot card reading and still practicing. Most people are happy to act as a "guinea pig" and provide you with feedback.

The Best Approach for Reading Cards for Others

Reading for others can be a shared exploration of the Tarot's symbolic help. The most productive approach that I have found for doing readings for others involves:

- encouraging verbalization of the questioner's impressions of the spread
- empowering the questioner to learn lessons and seek new solutions through the Tarot
- emphasizing the psychological and spiritual aspects of the issue rather than events only
- clarifying the role of the Tarot as a tool for inner growth rather than an infallible predictive oracle
- reminding the questioner that you are acting as the interpreter of her own unconscious mind
- reassuring the questioner when challenging cards appear and offering hope and inspiration regarding difficult processes.

What If You Are Expected to Predict?

Dispelling the expectation of prediction is the most problematic aspect of reading for others because it is so inextricably linked to the idea of Tarot card reading. You might preface your reading for another person by saying that you use the cards more for insight than prediction. Since we each have free will, we can change the direction of future events through our decisions and growth. The events shown in a Tarot spread only represent the *tendency* for events to go this way or that – not a certainty.

For example, a person may be having money problems and ask for information from the Tarot about that situation. You may see financial relief coming up ahead. If you just say that money looks good in the near future, the person may just wait for money to magically appear. Her discomfort about money may be because she has mis-managed her money and needs to learn how to be responsible about it. She may need to look for work or promote business opportunities to solve her financial problem. By noticing which Major Arcana cards have appeared in the spread, you can explain to her the underlying lessons that are involved in her difficulty.

Tact in Your Delivery

It is also very important to exercise tact and discretion when you are explaining your interpretation of a spread. I have tried to emphasize the positive qualities of all the cards in the interpretations given in this book. There will be times when several challenging cards appear in a spread and can provoke anxiety for both reader and questioner. There is never any reason to predict negative and fearful events but it is helpful to prepare a person for worsening conditions. Usually, when the stressful cards are very prominent in a spread, the questioner knows what is difficult and causing stress in her life. If you see that a painful situation is headed for closure or release, it is good to let the questioner know this and let her express her emotional response to it. Ask her which card strikes her as most representative of her situation or feelings about it.

By continually returning to your primary motivation of counseling another person rather than pontificating, you will avoid the pitfall of feeling you have to make predictions. Your role is to work with the questioner to delve into the Tarot symbols and discover how she can empower herself through awareness.

Focus on the Questioner

Many questions involve the lives of other people intertwined with the questioner's but at times people want you to probe the private lives of other people. This activity not only violates the privacy of others but takes the focus away from the questioner's responsibility and power over her own destiny. Often, the questioner wishes to manipulate other people by snooping on them with the aid of the Tarot cards. Gently suggest another approach to the issue or another way of phrasing the question to avoid this infringement of privacy. You might identify the underlying insecurity driving the questioner to want to probe in this way and address that need in a spread.

The Major Arcana

Overview

The Major Arcana cards are archetypes and express the deepest symbolic meanings of the Tarot. They represent the psychological and spiritual evolution of each person moving forward through lessons learned and wisdom gained. The Fool, for example, is connected to the archetype of innocence and fresh new beginnings. The Major Arcana cards in a spread refer to the meaning *behind* external events rather than everyday happenings themselves. However, some of the characters in the Major Arcana such as the Emperor, Empress, High Priestess, Hierophant, and others can represent important people in your life.

The best way to get acquainted with each Major Arcana card is to personalize its energy by associating it with your own personal feelings, experiences, dreams, or literary and film characters. In this way, you experience the flavor of each card and feel its energy from your own personal frame of reference. Gradually, you develop an intuitive sense about the essence of the card's meaning and feel that it has come alive for you.

For example, the Magician might conjure up the genius of Houdini, Einstein, or Merlin. Without these personal associations, you might be limited to an abstract intellectual approach to the Magician's creative intelligence. With your personal associations, the energy of the Magician comes to life and expresses his own unique vitality in action.

Many Major Arcana Cards Appearing in a Spread

If half or more of the cards in a spread are Major Arcana cards, there are levels to the question that are subtle and lie beneath the surface. Psychological and spiritual meanings are often more important in this case than the superficial events surrounding the question. In these instances, go over the meaning of each Major Arcana card in the spread carefully. Examine your hopes, fears, and expectations about the issues that feel challenging. Often, it takes much soul searching to understand the deeper revelations of the Major Arcana cards.

Meanings of the Major Arcana Cards

There are 22 cards in the Major Arcana, beginning with the Fool numbered 0 and progressing in consecutive order up to the World numbered XXI. A quick reference to their upright and reversed meanings follows:

0 Fool	naive; fresh, innocent approach; optimism; willing to take a chance
Reversed	too idealistic; Pollyanna; risky, foolish move; foolhardy
I Magician	enterprising, resourceful, inventive, intuitive ideas; independent strong-willed man; streak of genius
Reversed	inconsistent; erratic; unstable; rebellious; headstrong; domineering man; commitment phobia
II High Priestess	hidden powers; deep mystery; intriguing woman, reserved and secretive; inscrutable older woman
Reversed	intentional intrigue and secrecy; misuse of psychic powers; spying; not looking deep enough
III Empress	comfort; luxury; ease; generosity; abundance; the mother; prosperity; fertility
Reversed	laziness; excess; extravagance; promiscuity; hedonism; spoils other people
IV Emperor	father figure; authority; final decision maker; boss; law and order
Reversed	tyrant; egomaniac; arbitrary in decisions; domineering
V Hierophant	society's rules; rigid; dogmatic; in a rut; hidebound; mindless tradition; status quo; conventional; orthodox religion
Reversed	ready to break out of a rut; open to innovative, unconventional ideas
VI Lovers	relationship based on intense attraction; passion; karmic tie; choosing correct path
Reversed	jealous, possessive, devouring love; obsessive, immature reactions in love; destructive passion; choosing wrong path

VII Chariot	action; assertiveness; will power; drive and ambition; new car; trip
Reversed	reckless action; no respect for law and order; misuse of power; stepping on people on the way to the top; car trouble; scattered energy
VIII Strength	quiet confidence and self-reliance; ability to cope; good health
Reversed	show of strength with fear and insecurity behind it; fear of failure; physically drained
IX Hermit	serious; reclusive; introverted; spartan; discipline; teacher; study; inner guidance and wisdom
Reversed	paranoid; afraid of close relationship; too withdrawn; "I am a rock, I am an island"
X Wheel of Fortune	good luck; synchronicity; coincidences; sudden events
Reversed	bad luck; Murphy's law; "one thing after another"; petty annoyances; minor setbacks; ups and downs
XI Justice	karmic or legal justice; balanced judgment; appropriate resolution
Reversed	injustice; prejudice; bias; illegal activity; out of balance; wasted energy; overcompensation
XII Hanged Man	self-sacrifice; suspension; on hold; ambivalence; hiding your time
Reversed	ready for decision and action; life is off hold; "all systems go"
XIII Death	endings and beginnings; cooperating in reevaluation and revamping of situation
Reversed	resisting change and needed transformation; holding on to decaying conditions; forced change
XIV Temperance	here and now awareness; appropriate action; zen-like gift for diplomacy and timing; controlling eating, drinking, smoking, dieting, or spending
Reversed	impulsive; overreaction; poor sense of timing; no flow; out of sync; going on a binge

XV Devil	temptation; settling for safe, comfortable, easy situation but no growth; giving in to a weakness; backsliding; choosing a situation for the wrong reasons
Reversed	overcoming a weakness or temptation; overcoming inertia and stagnation
XVI Tower	plans fall apart; breakdown of false structure; false sense of security crumbles; unexpected shakeup in plans; surprising turn of events
Reversed	releasing a past mistake; acceptance of the necessary collapse of false security
XVII Star	dreams; meditation; visualization; optimism; sense of purpose; inspiring wishes and dreams; vision and hope for one's highest potential
Reversed	disillusionment; hopelessness; depression; pessimism; purposelessness; illness
XVIII Moon	psychic ability; dreams; behind the scene activity; unspoken messages; more than meets the eye
Reversed	subversive activity; psychic attack; sabotage; rip off; drugs; illegal acts; hidden things come to light; misunderstandings; being secretly undermined; bad vibrations
XIX Sun	honor; recognition; fulfillment of goals; success
Reversed	too much ego; showy; wanting to be center stage; content to look good but not earn success; pessimism; negativity; failure
XX Judgement	good karma; winning law suit; beginning of new cycle; reward for positive effect; reap what you have sown
Reversed	negative karma; losing law suit; punishment for failure to learn; lessons not yet learned; bad judgment
XXI World	mastery over a situation or field; international travel; able to handle all aspects well; completion; synthesis
Reversed	limited understanding of the situation; not seeing total picture; unfinished business; almost ready for completion and a new cycle

0 THE FOOL
(Innocence)

UPRIGHT MEANING: The Fool is numbered 0 because he represents both the beginning and the end of the journey through the 21 stages of spiritual growth through the Major Arcana cards. He is pictured as a jester dancing on the edge of a precipice because he symbolizes a childlike sense of awe and wonder about new adventures ahead. He relies primarily on his instincts represented by the dog playing at his heels. The sun shines brightly overhead reflecting his optimism and crystals spring from the earth at his feet showing his connection to the mystical realms. He is inexperienced about the pitfalls that he may encounter, but his innocence allows him to see life as fresh and full of fascination. His sense of humor allows him to poke fun at the foolishness of himself and others without malice. He lives in the moment with a sense of playfulness bringing a lightness to his perception of life. He avoids planning too far ahead or worrying about the future. His spontaneity instinctively guides him to the experiences he needs. He believes that life should be fun and expects each day to bring new wonders for his enjoyment.

Related Examples: Peter Pan, Scarecrow (The Wizard of Oz), Puck

IN A SPREAD: When the Fool appears in a spread, he often signifies a readiness for a new path in life, one that brings feelings of excitement and anticipation. The Minor Arcana suit that predominates will provide information about whether the new direction is primarily creative, emotional, mental, or financial. By trusting in fresh ideas and a sense of playfulness, you will be led to begin a cycle of renewal — one that will expand your sense of freedom and creative exploration. With the **World**, the **Prince of Wands**, or the **6 of Swords**, the Fool can indicate travel.

REVERSED MEANING: You may be in danger of letting naivete and wishful thinking impede your judgment. Your actions may be premature or impulsive. Think carefully about the realistic ramifications of any decisions you are considering.

I THE MAGICIAN
(Innovation)

UPRIGHT MEANING: The Magician is pictured with the symbol of infinity at his third eye chakra radiating the light of intuition. Below him is a table holding four tools at his disposal: the Sword of intellect, the Wand of inspiration, the Cup of emotion, and the Pentacle of practicality. Because he is guided by the light of his intuitive mind, he combines the energies of the tools with originality. He values freedom and independence and may be considered eccentric by those of limited vision. The Magician is adept at applying the universal laws of manifestation and may be impatient with the slower processes of society. He prefers to follow the dictates of his creative genius even though he may be considered a maverick by society. He has difficulty answering to anyone's authority but his own, unless his work allows flexibility and autonomy. His interests are often unusual and progressive, possibly involving metaphysics or high technology. His original vision often leads him to explore inventions.

Related Examples: Houdini, Nickola Tesla, Ross Perot

IN A SPREAD: When the Magician appears in a spread, the ability to manifest your wishes through creative visualization is heightened. The surrounding cards may reflect the likely direction for your originality and intuition. You may notice more synchronicity or "meaningful coincidences" going on around you. A person who embodies much of the unconventional qualities of the Magician may enter your life to mirror for you the expression of your own unique gifts.

REVERSED MEANING: The Magician reversed can indicate the misuse of creative talents or the expression of freedom and eccentricity at the expense of others. Political radicals and crackpots often fall into this category as well as talented people whose fame has "gone to their heads." It shows a person whose fascination with their own ideas or talent has blinded them to how they fit into society as a whole. With the **Devil** or the **Moon**, it can relate to intentional manipulation of others or black magic.

II THE HIGH PRIESTESS
(Psychic Powers)

UPRIGHT MEANING: The High Priestess appears as the beautiful face of Greta Garbo surrounded by symbols of mystery and femininity. The yin/yang symbol at her third eye signifies her ability to blend active and passive energies as she expresses her deep intuitive powers. The moon and the ocean are symbols of her emotional depth and sensitivity. The alpha and omega in the book pictured suggest the limitlessness of the wisdom available to her. She wears a veil over her eyes to show the mysteries she uncovers with her penetrating gaze. She symbolizes the person who is able to plumb the depths of life through a natural intuitive perceptiveness. She may also explore psychology, divinatory tools, dream work, music, or dance to enhance her exploration of the subtle realms. Her psychic powers and natural empathy can make her an exceptional counselor. She needs time to turn inward regularly and record her dreams or journal her deepest thoughts.

Related Examples: Isis, the Oracle at Delphi, Fairy Godmother

IN A SPREAD: When this card appears in a spread next to favorable cards, your psychic abilities are strong, implying that what you *sense* may be more reliable than what you *think* about a situation. A psychic, perceptive woman or man such as the person described above may enter your life to encourage your own inner exploration. It may be a good time to take a Tarot or dream interpretation class or to explore deep feelings through journaling or therapy.

REVERSED MEANING: You may not be looking deep enough into your own unconscious for answers or may be blocking your feelings out of fear. Next to a Court Card, a person around you may be manipulative or underhanded. When combined with the **Moon** or the **7 of Cups**, your psychic perceptions may be clouded. Wait until a sense of clarity dispels some of the paranoia and confusion you may be experiencing.

III THE EMPRESS
(Fertility)

UPRIGHT MEANING: The Empress is pictured as a regal woman, wearing a crown and jewels. The five-pointed star around her neck symbolizes her connection to humanity while the planet earth and the bird represent her role as Earth Mother or Gaia. She embodies the nurturing and abundance that we receive when we connect with nature. She is a symbol of verdant fertility and abundant resources. The Empress expresses the feminine principle at its most domestic in her love of home, family, delicious food, and luxury. She is the essence of elegance and beauty and shares her generous bounty with all who come into contact with her. She enjoys cultural events and social interactions and is likely to be active in the community. Her philosophy is one of prosperity and enjoyment of sensual pleasures for she is connected to the power of all to attract what is needed in order to flourish.

Related Examples: Venus de Milo, Betty Crocker, southern belle

IN A SPREAD: When the Empress appears in a spread, you are ready to accept greater prosperity into your life. If you feel deserving of abundant resources and growth and expect to receive what you need, the Empress can signal the arrival of greater bounty in your life. Your family may grow if the Empress appears with the **3 of Cups** signifying a pregnancy. An elegant and expansive person may enter your life mirroring for you the abundance you are ready to attract. Spend some time enjoying nature or pamper your self with a massage or long bath.

REVERSED MEANING: When reversed, the Empress can signify extravagance, laziness, self-indulgence, and superficiality. You may be overextended financially or feeling overweight and out-of-shape. Status symbols and rich food may have seduced you away from a healthy contact with nature and a simpler life style. Examine how voluntary simplicity and moderation might bring areas of your life back into balance. Re-examine how you give of yourself to others and look for ways that you can promote their growth.

IV THE EMPEROR
(Order)

UPRIGHT MEANING: The Emperor is pictured seated on a throne wearing a crown with the wand and orb of power in his lap. He symbolizes rulership through law and order. His kingdom is based on structure, logic, and rules. He is the symbol of authority, whether as a father, corporate executive, government official, or community leader. The stone tower in the background represents the ability to organize ideas into structures and hierarchies to accomplish tasks. The left-brain, linear process of completing projects is related to the Emperor. Psychologically, he relates to your maturity and ability to assume responsibility and the way you experienced your personal father and authority figures in general.

Related Examples: George Washington, Queen Elizabeth I, Henry Kissinger

IN A SPREAD: The appearance of the Emperor in a spread can signal a strong foundation and sense of order coming into your life. He may represent the necessity for you to deal with the laws and rules of society by interfacing with the government or civil authority. The Emperor can indicate authority figures who can be helpful through their expertise about practical spheres of influence. You might seek information from such a resource in order to have a firm grounding for new undertakings.

REVERSED MEANING: The Emperor reversed symbolizes misuse of power which can manifest as tyranny or corruption. A person in authority may be abusive, domineering, and arbitrary. When this card represents a person, he often hides his insecurity by intimidating and abusing others.

V THE HIEROPHANT
(Spiritual Ritual)

UPRIGHT MEANING: The Hierophant is dressed in the robes of a Pope showing his connection to spiritual ritual. He holds a Tarot card in his hand and projects wisdom and clarity in a stream of light from his right eye. Representatives of the Jewish, Catholic, Muslim, and Metaphysical religious traditions approach him, signifying the ecumenical nature of his message. His approach to spirituality is one of adherence to traditional religious beliefs and rituals rather than an independent and personal relationship with God. He fosters the structure of formal church services and the unity of his congregation. He may become dogmatic about his particular choice of belief systems and refuse to acknowledge the truth of other viewpoints.

Related Examples: Billy Graham, the Pope, full moon meditation

IN A SPREAD: The Hierophant most often relates to the role of religion in your life, but can also relate to traditional values and attitudes. The Hierophant can show an area of your life where you are conservative and conditoned by society. You might need to re-examine whether you agree with the traditional mindset you have adopted. If you are engaged in performing "empty" rituals because you feel it is expected of you, you might create rituals of your own to express your authentic connection to your spiritual life.

REVERSED MEANING: The Hierophant reversed shows a readiness to break out of a rut and shatter outworn habits. You may feel ready to break with tradition and free yourself from past conditioning. When this card appears, you are ready to re-evaluate any area where you feel you are on "automatic pilot", because you will feel increasing dissatisfaction without change.

VI THE LOVERS
(Powerful Attraction)

UPRIGHT MEANING: In this card, a man and woman embrace, connected through their hearts to a cord of energy from the yin/yang symbol of the attraction of opposites. The Star of David above unites the feminine triangle of involution with the masculine triangle of evolution, symbolizing the balance possible through the union of the sexes. In Jungian psychology, the animus is the unconscious male side of a woman's psyche and the anima is the unconscious female side of a man's psyche. The Lovers relate to the powerful attraction that can result when our animus or anima is stimulated by the other person. Our ideal "other half" can inspire intoxicating feelings or even obsession when we fall in love. The couple are pictured in a beautiful scene in nature signifying the power of sexual attraction to manifest fertility in the natural world.

Related Examples: Romeo and Juliet, Rhett and Scarlett

IN A SPREAD: The Lovers in a spread most often applies to a powerful physical attraction to another person, combined with a deep and often mystifying spiritual bond. There may be past-life karma with the other person that accounts for the instant recognition and fascination you are experiencing. You may share an easy, comfortable rapport and almost a telepathic bond with one another. The Lovers can also signify difficult choices in life where you may be influenced by a powerful attraction to a certain direction.

REVERSED MEANING: The attraction may be primarily physical and addictive with the Lovers reversed. This card describes couples who thrive on the intensity of conflict and the euphoria of making up. Because it is difficult for the couple to understand their destructive obsession with one another, this type of relationship is often most difficult to release. There may be difficult but hidden karmic issues between them binding them together. When this card relates to a difficult life choice, you may be obsessively attracted to a particular direction, but for unhealthy reasons.

VII THE CHARIOT
(Motivation)

UPRIGHT MEANING: In the Chariot card, a powerful man controls the reins of an elaborate chariot pulled by two racing horses. The horses symbolize instinct and their black and white colors represent the duality which the charioteer must master in order to focus his energies on his goals. The charioteer wears the symbol for the sign Cancer on his solar plexus, showing mastery of his emotions as he controls his instincts. People who resonate to the Chariot have high energy, motivation, and a focused will and may gravitate to careers as salepeople or entrepreneurs. The Chariot also relates to strong, athletic, and travel-oriented people, who thrive on physical challenges and adventure. Cars, motorcycles, machines, and travel by car also express the energy of the Chariot.

Related Example: Indiana Jones, Hans Solo, Rambo, Rocky

IN A SPREAD: You are ready to proceed with will, energy, and momentum toward your goals. Your motivation will sustain you when the process becomes tedious. You feel physically strong and may enjoy outdoor activities, especially in conjunction with a short trip. With the **Ace of Pentacles** or the **Empress**, the timing could be right for buying a new car. A person embodying the high energy and motivation of the Chariot may express the confidence you are ready to integrate into your life.

REVERSED MEANING: The Chariot reversed shows selfish and ruthless misuse of the will, with the attitude of a spoiled brat. A brash and insensitive demeanor can alienate others and trigger anger and retaliation. A person with these personality traits may be creating turmoil for you. It may be necessary to have a confrontation about this behavior or remove yourself from the abusive situation. With the **Tower, Ace of Swords R**, or **3 of Swords**, this person could become violent. Energy directed toward projects may be too scattered to be effective. Go back to your priorities and eliminate unnecessary distractions. With cards of financial loss, the Chariot reversed can indicate car trouble.

VIII JUSTICE
(Balance)

UPRIGHT MEANING: The crowned woman with the clear-seeing eye of the eagle projects right judgement in a stream of insight from both eyes. Springing from the rose of compassion is a scales with the sign Libra on its stem, signifying fairness blended with mercy as the ideal of the Justice card. Other symbols of balance in the card are day and night behind the woman's head, the yin/yang symbol on her breast, and the upper and lower triangles of the Star of David being weighed in the scales. The Justice card relates to balance in karmic terms as well as legal terms. The blending of wisdom and compassion are necessary to judge properly. When King Solomon offered to cut a child in half who was claimed by two different mothers, he used his gift for loving wisdom to recognize that the true mother would not want the child harmed. Often, achieving balance in legal, karmic, and interpersonal arenas of life requires a sense of what conscience dictates rather than the "letter of the law."

Related Examples: Perry Mason, Ralph Nader, Robert Kennedy

IN A SPREAD: The Justice card can indicate legal matters at hand and with favorable cards, a decision in your favor. With cards relating to other matters, it can indicate a proper balance and right attitudes about your needs versus those of others. In matters of health, a sense of proportion in your lifestyle and diet improves your well-being.

REVERSED MEANING: Justice reversed indicates an imbalance, injustice, or lack of proportion in some area of your life. In a pending legal matter, you may lose the case or be treated unfairly. Examine whether the balance between what you give to others and receive from them is fair to both parties. With the **6 of Pentacles R** or the **7 of Pentacles R**, debts may be creating an imbalance in your life. Avoid feeling emotionally obligated to rescue someone who has lessons to learn about balance.

IX THE HERMIT
(Guidance)

UPRIGHT MEANING: The Hermit is pictured meditating with his body twisted into a yoga asana position. He wears the symbol of the "OHM" in a band across his third eye and garments displaying the astrological symbols of the Sun, Jupiter, and Virgo. A bright star in the night sky illuminates both a mountaintop behind him and a lantern at his feet. He is the seeker of inner wisdom and illumination gained from a solitary life of quiet reflection. He studies esoteric subjects such as astrology and meditation and incorporates their insights into his life. He may teach others the lessons he has learned on his own personal quest but resists becoming another's guru. He trusts his inner guidance for the answers in his life and encourages others to access their own source of insight. He prefers to live simply without emphasis on material or sensual wants. He enjoys scholarly research into the meaning and purpose of life and treasures the books that have expanded his wisdom.

Related Examples: Matthex Fox, Yogananda, Mother Theresa, Thoreau

IN A SPREAD: When the Hermit appears in your spread, you may feel harried with everyday concerns and need privacy and time to reflect. Meditation and journaling will help move your thoughts inward. Spiritual reading can inspire you and help you put events into perspective. You may seek education about a subject of interest to you or go on a spiritual retreat. A spiritual teacher or counselor could offer valuable insights.

REVERSED MEANING: When reversed, the Hermit can mean too much time alone and more need for social contact. You may be feeling lonely and out of step with the world. After a necessary period of solitude following a health problem or the break-up of a relationship, this card can signal a completion of a "hermit" phase and a need to return to a more active life style. If the period of solitude has been extended, you may have some fear of allowing people to share your time' or space.

X WHEEL OF FORTUNE
(Changing Cycles)

UPRIGHT MEANING: The wheels within wheels pictured on the Wheel of Fortune relate to interwoven astrological influences and kabbalistic symbols as they reflect the changing cycles in our lives. The Wheel of Fortune reminds us that fate, destiny, and luck are factors that affect us all and that our inner cycles are moving us constantly toward growth. Astrology, numerology, and biorhythms put us in touch with the shifting experiences and lessons our Soul is seeking. Recognizing and accepting the inevitability of the "ups and downs" of life is one of the key ideas symbolized by the Wheel of Fortune. Chance often has a greater impact on us than causality when we encounter synchronistic events that put us in touch with the "hand of the universe" in our lives.

Related Examples: I Ching, stock market, bio-rhythms, seasons

IN A SPREAD: You may be in a period of good luck when this card appears with other favorable cards. You are ready to take some chances with your life by following the dreams that fill you with excitement and enthusiasm. You may drawn toward gambling or speculation and feel optimistic about taking risks. The advice of an astrologer or numerologist could help you see the best use of a lucky cycle.

REVERSED: The Wheel of Fortune reversed describes jangled, chaotic events and the feeling that difficulties are mounting in your life. You could be unlucky with risk-taking or out of step with your intuitive sense of good timing. You may need to wait until an astrological cycle changes, such as Mercury retrograde going direct, before you feel more flowing energy.

XI STRENGTH
(Healing)

UPRIGHT MEANING: A nude woman with a cobra design on her tiara holds a piece of fabric decorated with the face of a lion. She appears to be at home in nature, loving her connection to the natural landscape and wild animals. The Strength card relates to the ability to comfort and heal others by using natural substances from nature and by gently encouraging others to acknowledge old emotional wounds. The strength expressed by this card is not so much physical brawn as a quiet sense of conviction and reliance upon natural law to cope with life's challenges. Alternative healers and therapies such as massage, acupuncture, homeopathy, and aromatherapy relate to the energy of this card.

Related Examples: Adelle Davis, Deepak Chopra, Edward Bach, Gandhi

IN A SPREAD: With the **Sun**, **Star**, or **4 of Swords R**, this card indicates good health or recovery from illness. Your energy is strong and you feel vital and capable. You may benefit from a hike in the woods or contact with animals at this time. With the **Hermit**, you may want to study natural healing techniques.

REVERSED MEANING: The reversed Strength card shows that your reserves of energy are low and you may need to boost your immune system to avoid becoming run down. Vitamins, herbs, or flower essences can help restore the balance. You may be feeling insecure about a challenging situation in your life and become aggressive to cover your fear. It is better to wait until your energies have recharged before tackling intimidating situations.

XII THE HANGED MAN
(Suspension)

UPRIGHT MEANING: The Hanged Man hangs with his hands folded suspended by his foot from the branch of a tree. A halo surrounds his head indicating that he is in a sacred space and his suspension is of his own choosing since no cord or rope binds him in this awkward position. The Hanged Man as card 12 marks the midway point in the Tarot deck. In the process of inner growth, it signifies that the Fool has become aware of his spiritual nature and is waiting for his life to shift to reflect that insight. There may be an extended period of time during which the Hanged Man feels finished with his old life but remains emotionally flat and ambivalent about new directions. He is forced to wait in suspended animation, unable to find any joy in returning to his old life, but confused about his future direction. On an inner level, this process is one of self-sacrifice and trust while the Soul repolarizes and reorients the person toward his spiritual purpose. Prior to this period in life, the person is getting his bearings in the material world and learning survival skills.

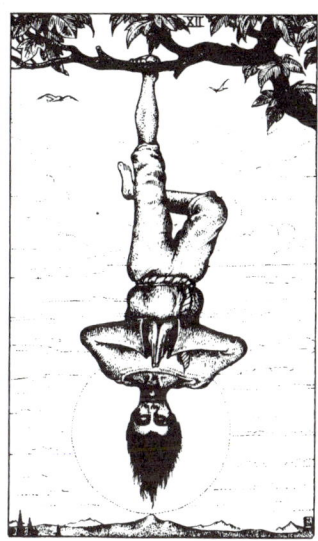

Related Examples: Christ, Osiris, Leonard Pelletier, Nelson Mandela

IN A SPREAD: The Hanged Man in a spread shows that you are "waiting for Godot" in some area of your life. If you can accept the fact that you may have to sacrifice your will to a situation over which you have no control, you may find this time period less painful. The ambivalence you feel may be even more poignant if the **2 of Swords** or **8 of Swords** are also in the spread. Ask for inner guidance about how you can spend this time most wisely and where your life will lead you next. When another person's actions directly impact your desire for a healthy lifestyle, such as living with an alcoholic spouse, this card can show your victimization resulting from the continuing abuse.

REVERSED MEANING: The reversed Hanged Man signifies that your period of waiting is over and you are ready to move ahead in your new life direction. External situations that have controlled your life no longer have the power to block your progress.

XIII DEATH
(Transformation)

UPRIGHT MEANING: The Death card shows the specter of death as a skeleton holding a sickle in one hand and a raven in the other. Tombstones crumble at his feet and strewn about him are symbols of the transitory nature of man's world — a clock, shattered sword, crumbling crown, and staring skulls. These ominous symbols rarely foretell physical death but instead convey the necessity to release the past and process the grief that accompanies it. Only by experiencing the death of an old self-image or phase of our lives can we feel the inner transformation required for our renewal. Sometimes, Death refers to a situation or relationship in our lives that has become stagnant or dysfunctional. An honest reevaluation and acceptance of the need for change is often what is called for to allow a natural transition into renewal. The Death card challenges us to look at our attachments and to realize that no matter how much we may deny the reality of any death experience in our lives, we can only suffer more when we delay a transformation that is overdue in our lives.

Related Examples: Elizabeth Kubler-Ross, Raymond Moody, Good Friday and Easter Sunday, near death experiences, AIDS epidemic

IN A SPREAD: This card may provoke fear when you see it in a spread until you learn to blend its meaning of transformation with the surrounding cards to learn on what level the ending and renewal need to happen. Notice which Minor Arcana suit predominates and which Major Arcana cards appear for clues to where you may be holding on too tightly to the past. The Death card can be a good indicator that you are cooperating with a release in your life, such as stopping an unhealthy habit.

REVERSED: Death reversed shows an unwillingness to face some necessary changes or endings. If you know you need to let go of something inhibiting to you but can't muster the will to let go, ask for guidance about how you can allow the willingness to change to embrace your life.

XIV TEMPERANCE
(Moderation)

UPRIGHT MEANING: The woman pictured on the Temperance card stands by a pool of water and pours water back and forth between two chalices. She is dressed in exotic attire and looks away as she pours the liquid. Her actions symbolize the perfect blending of energies that can occur when we trust intuition to guide us in our words and actions. She does not need to measure the amount of water she is pouring to know how much is right. In the same way, we can sense the right timing for our actions and make aesthetic choices that suit our taste. Temperance often applies to the ability to mix different elements in pleasing proportions, as good cooks and artists demonstrate so well. The mindfulness to stay in the present and respond authentically to life is symbolized by the Temperance card, as well as a moderate and balanced lifestyle.

Related Examples: Weight Watchers, Greco-Roman art, Lean Cuisine

IN A SPREAD: You have learned to stay in the moment and trust the timing of events as they unfold. Your ability to follow your instincts regarding dietary, artistic, and purchasing choices will continue to bring satisfaction. The Temperance card with the **Devil R** or **Justice** could be helpful for dieting or bringing excesses under control because you are attuned now to what your body needs.

REVERSED MEANING: You may be feeling impatient and want to rush situations. Meditation can help you return to the "here and now" consciousness that will put you in sync with proper timing. If you are prone to binging in times of stress, you could be throwing your system out of balance. Artistic pursuits or cooking could relieve the pressure and provide an outlet for your intuitive side.

XV THE DEVIL
(Temptation)

UPRIGHT MEANING: The Devil depicts a horned creature dressed in a business suit with an inverted pentagram suspended from his neck holding several men and women captive. He wears a ring through his nose to show the beastiality of his nature while the inverted pentagram signifies misuse of will or black magic. A guard tower in the background signifies the imprisonment of the captives. The Devil refers to those weaknesses or addictions that hold the greatest fascination for us. They may have served us well as a coping mechanism when we were less aware, but we know deep down that they will keep us from our growth if we persist. The Devil can refer to addiction to a substance, workaholism, sexual addiction, or codependency. It often manifests as greed, especially in our society where a person's self-esteem is so linked to his material possessions. The temptations symbolized by the Devil card are especially seductive to us when we feel vulnerable or fearful. They lure us into the false belief that the weakness or addiction will make us stronger by bolstering our courage. In reality, the backsliding only serves to create another problem to resolve.

Related Examples: Rasputin, Gordon Gecko (Wall Street), Darth Vader

IN A SPREAD: You may be tempted at this time to break good resolutions you have made. If you are in recovery from an addiction, this is the time to go back to the Twelve Steps for inspiration. You are at a new phase of the old addictive cycle in which you have the opportunity to make new choices when you feel discouraged or vulnerable. Re-examine decisions based on purely materialistic motives. A person of questionable ethics may be trying to seduce you with the promise of quick money.

REVERSED MEANING: Here, you see the futility of continuing to behave self-destructively. You recognize the familiar seductive voice in your head urging you to backslide or take the easy road. You have learned the lesson regarding your greatest weakness or "addiction of choice" and are accepting the new growth you have earned. You resist unhealthy influences from others and are not caught up in material desires.

XVI THE TOWER
(Catalyst for Change)

UPRIGHT MEANING: A stone tower is pictured blasted apart while the occupants and their earthly crown fall to the ground. A heavenly intelligence looks down radiating sudden enlightment. The Tower card appears dire and disruptive but often it refers to a situation that has become stagnant or dysfunctional and calls for change. A needed catalyst may shake up the situation, such as an accident, separation, bankruptcy, or emotional crisis. Often, the disruptive event happens without warning, leaving us in shock for a period of time. Through the disorienting event, we are able to see our priorities in a new light and put the pieces of our life back together. Our new awareness will help us to choose a new and more appropriate structure for our future.

Related Examples: volcanic destruction of Pompeii, fall of Atlantis, stock market crash of 1929, Watergate

IN A SPREAD: The surrounding cards will reveal the area of your life most affected by the upset - finances with Pentacles, feelings with Cups, mental stress with Swords, or spirituality and inspiration with Wands. With the **Chariot R**, an auto accident could be indicated. With the **Wheel of Fortune**, the **Sun**, or the **Empress**, the surprise could be a lucky break or surprising opportunity.

REVERSED MEANING: When reversed, the Tower refers to untenable circumstances that you know must collapse. You have "seen the handwriting on the wall" and know that the disruption is inevitable and must be accepted. By cooperating with the needed change in your life, you can incorporate the enlightenment gained from your ordeal into your plans for the future.

XVII THE STAR
(Sense of Purpose)

UPRIGHT MEANING: Under the light of the moon, a nude woman wading in a stream pours water from two chalices back into the stream. A bright star above reflects on a location in the distance and illuminates the star at her crown chakra. A flamingo drinks from one of her cups. A waterfall cascades in the background. The many watery symbols in the Star card reflect the desire and inspiration that we feel when we connect to our inner purpose and heart's desire. The crown chakra connects each of us to the clear knowing of our Divine Intuition. From this source, we can connect to our deepest source of joy and our hopes and dreams. The Star can represent acting, musical, or artistic talent and with cards of fame can relate to movie stars. Star gazers, whether they are astrologers, astronomers, or UFO trackers respond to the energy of the Star card.

Related Examples: Mary Poppins, Jonathan Livingston Seagull, The Little Engine That Could, wishing wells, rock stars,

IN A SPREAD: You are connected to your deepest hopes and could benefit from visualizing your dreams and expecting them to manifest. You would benefit from movies, plays, or literature that inspire you to follow your dreams. Your creative talents will bring you increasing fulfillment as you allow yourself to enjoy playful activities. Your health is strong and your state of mind is optimistic.

REVERSED MEANING: You may feel hopeless and depressed with little inspiration in your life presently. Your health may be suffering if the **8 of Swords**, **4 of Swords**, or **Sun R** also appear in the spread. Connect to the issues that are dampening your spirits and resolve your feelings of disappointment about past losses. By letting yourself "bottom out" emotionally, you will be able to return to your source of inspiration and hope for the future.

XVIII THE MOON
(Hidden Forces)

UPRIGHT MEANING: Under the light of a full moon in which the two fish symbolizing Pisces swim, a lobster creeps from a dark pool of water onto the earth. He seems to be drawn toward the rays of moonlight that descend to earth. These symbols express the mysterious areas of the psyche that we often repress - our fears, guilt, hidden animosities, or psychic impressions. Our unconscious mind can impinge on our everyday consciousness through vague foreboding feelings, paranoia, or disturbing dreams. We may want to ignore the information and dismiss it as confusing or meaningless but the unconscious will become more persistent until it is heard. The purpose of this prodding from our hidden self is to make us more self-aware so that our unconscious and conscious minds cooperate with one another. By paying attention to the messages of our hunches, misgivings, and dreams, we receive help that only our "right brain" or intuition can give us to deepen our perceptions.

Related Examples: Carl Jung, Alcoholics Anonymous, CIA, past lives

IN A SPREAD: You may be feeling confused and disturbed by unsettling influences around you. Miscommunications are likely but may be unintentional. Your fears may be working overtime creating exaggerated reactions to minor annoyances. You may be projecting selfish motives onto other people because of unresolved issues with people from your past. Your dreams could be disturbing but also serve to clear up emotional residue.

REVERSED MEANING: There may be negative energy in your environment that needs clearing out through visualizing white light or burning sage. Pay attention to any hunches you get about selfish or manipulative motives of those around you who may appear trustworthy. People around you may be engaged in dishonest or illegal acts. Ask for a dream to clarify your misgivings. You may have to keep your perceptions to yourself until you have more of a factual basis for sharing them with others. Hidden activities will come to light and you will see the validity of your intuitions.

XIX THE SUN
(Joy)

UPRIGHT MEANING: The Sun radiates its energizing light overhead as a child enjoys the pleasures of a paradise-like garden. The Sun card symbolizes an infectious zest for life. When we project energy, vitality, and enjoyment of each moment, people love to be in our presence and return our happiness in kind. The confidence and joy reflected in the Sun card are not based on inexperience or naivete, as in the Fool card. The 19th card in the Tarot shows the progression of the Fool through many challenges and experiences to come to the full expression of his true inner being. He knows that he has a unique spark of the Divine within him and relishes sharing his creativity and vision with others. He encourages those he encounters to joyously express their special gifts.

Related Examples: Robin Williams, King Arthur, Richard Simmons, Hillary Clinton

IN A SPREAD: You are in touch with your creativity and optimism about the future. Being in the outdoors soaking up the sunshine brings you joy and energy. You have honored your "inner child" and are not afraid of looking silly when you express your humor and playfulness. You are in a position to attract recognition and success in your endeavors.

REVERSED MEANING: Here, pessimism and lack of confidence is blocking your success. Being out in the sun in nature may help lighten your spirits. Your energy may feel low and you may feel ill or depressed, especially if **Strength R**, the **8 of Swords**, **9 of Swords**, or the **10 of Swords** are also in the spread. Look for ways to energize yourself through grounding in nature, yoga, massage, dance, or creative activities.

XX JUDGEMENT
(Reward)

UPRIGHT MEANING: The Judgement card pictures angels trumpets overhead sounding the Day of Judgement while resurrected people arise joyously from the earth. These symbols show the awakening to the union of the soul with the personality that this card expresses. The Fool has now come to the full realization that he is connected to all sentient beings in the universe and therefore cannot break Universal Law without hurting himself. He has rectified any karmic imbalances and is reborn into his identification with his Higher Self. He is able to exercise good judgement guided by ethics and integrity in his dealings with others and is ready to begin a new cycle of expansion of awareness.

Related Examples. Ralph Waldo Emerson, Buddha, Luke Skywalker

IN A SPREAD: You have learned some very important lessons recently about making decisions from a spiritual perspective. You have exercised wisdom in making your spiritual growth your first priority. You may feel as if you have been reborn on some level and have left behind an old identity. You have learned to think in terms of both parties "winning" rather than one winning and the other losing in solving everyday problems. With the **5 of Wands R**, **Justice**, and the **5 of Swords R**, a lawsuit may be decided in your favor.

REVERSED MEANING: When reversed, the Judgement card shows insufficient clarity about your highest motivations to make good decisions at this time. You may be dealing with the ramifications of old decisions you made that were poorly thought out. Rather than focusing on the punitive side of the situation, you might view the karmic imbalance you are now experiencing as helping to show you how you can make better decisions in your life. Review your karmic obligations to others and to society and look for ways that you can come from your highest motives in all your dealings with others. Instead of a Win Lose approach to life, seek Win-Win solutions to problems. Legal matters may be problematic or unsuccessful at this time.

XXI THE WORLD
(Synthesis)

UPRIGHT MEANING: In the picture on this card, a woman holding a wand dances on top of the world with flowers growing at her feet. She is surrounded by the symbols for the four fixed signs of the zodiac: Taurus the bull, Leo the lion, Scorpio the eagle, and Aquarius the enlightened man. The woman symbolizes mastery of the attachments that the fixed signs express: the attraction of Taurus for sensuality and possessions, the craving of Leo for adulation and flashiness, the desire of Scorpio for sex, money, and power, and the fascination of Aquarius with revolution and eccentricity. When we have mastered the polarization that attachment creates, we are ready to allow all experiences to move through us without attachment. The World is a card of synthesis because it shows the ability to blend different elements of a subject together into a cohesive whole. As the last card in the Tarot, it represents mastery of all the steps and processes that the Fool has encountered on his quest.

Related Examples: United Nations, world peace, global ecology, cultural diversity, international travel

IN A SPREAD: You are at a point of completion with a situation in your life and have synthesized and mastered the lessons needed in that experience. The wisdom you have gained from completing those lessons will serve you well in similar experiences in the future. You may wish to broaden your horizons now through extensive or long distance travel, if the **Fool**, **6 of Swords**, **Prince of Wands**, or the **Wheel of Fortune** also appear in the spread.

REVERSED MEANING: You may have a nagging feeling of unfinished business about a situation that you have been learning from for sometime. You are ready to integrate the few remaining insights necessary for you to feel clear about completion and move on. Ask for inner guidance or a dream to help synthesize the remaining pieces of the puzzle. A long distance trip may be delayed, if other travel cards are also reversed.

THE UNKNOWABLE
(Hidden Information)

MEANING: The Unknowable card is an optional card that can be added to the Tarot deck to represent the secrets we keep from ourselves during a reading. Many decks have extra cards included with the pack that have the same design on the back as the rest of the deck. The Cosmic Tarot deck has an extra card that says "Quality since 1860" that can be used for this purpose. Even with a tool as vast as the Tarot, there are finite limits to the information accessible through it. Sometimes, we are not meant to know certain things ahead of time. Having preconceived notions about the outcome of certain situations can remove us from the present moment and diminish the wonder of unraveling the future as it progresses. When the Unknowable card appears in a spread, it acts as a signal that our question involves information that we are not yet meant to know. The meanings of the other cards in the spread can be interpreted, but the presence of the Unknowable card alerts us that we have entered uncharted territory in the reading. The best guidance in these situations is our intuitive prompting about what feels right for the next step ahead. Because we are venturing into a new area of growth, we must have faith and rely upon our instincts to see us through. After a week or so, or whenever the surrounding conditions have changed, the cards can be consulted again about the same situation. If the Unknowable card is missing in the spread, more clarity is available about the issue. When the Unknowable card appears repeatedly when consulting the Tarot, it shows that only limited input about the future is helpful at that time. It may indicate a need to express and process feelings rather than focus on outcomes.

The Minor Arcana

Overview

The Minor Arcana of the Tarot consists of four suits with 14 cards in each numbered from the Ace to the King. Brief descriptions of the meaning of each card of the Minor Arcana by suit is included in this chapter for easy reference. More detailed descriptions are arranged numerically beginning with the next chapter, so that learning the meanings of each card can be associated with its number. The Ace's, Two's, Three's etc. are grouped together to simplify learning the meaning of each.

Swords

Swords involve tension, the force of will, and confrontation. They express mental energy, turmoil, and anxiety. Upright and reversed meanings of the individual Sword cards are described below.

ACE	A forceful beginning fueled by courage and willfulness; standing up for a cause; determination; strong sense of conviction
Reversed	Pushing too hard; forcing the issue; browbeating others; aggressive show of power
2	Ambivalent; indecisive; stuck in a stalemate; uneasy truce
Reversed	Stalemate resolved; decisions reached; clarity of mind after difficult dilemma
3	Jealousy; envy; competition in a relationship; intense attachment with control issues; separation, divorce, heartbreak; power struggle
Reversed	Intensity and pain easing; jealousy and envy subsiding; getting over a breakup or painful relationship
4	need for recuperation from stress; sickness; inactivity; rest from conflict; calm, quiet healing; rest and recuperation
Reversed	healing is over; ready for activity; restoration of health; recuperation complete
5	gloating enemy; unfaithful lover; jealous vindictive enemy; vicious gossip; betrayal; lack of forgiveness
Reversed	vindication and triumph over enemy and over gossip and betrayal; forgiveness
6	helpful assistance in strife; turmoil subsiding; problems can be worked out; bridge over troubled waters; travel over water
Reversed	heading for trouble again; no immediate solution; help not accepted

7		theft; bitterness over rip off; feeling like a loser in contest; victimized; mistrust
	Reversed	return of stolen property or person; unexpected triumph after a loss
8		restriction and limitation; no understanding of blocks to freedom; refusal to break chains
	Reversed	breaking out of prison; unblocking fear of independence; seeing path to escape; overcoming outside restriction
9		worry and anxiety over worsening problems; heavy grief or depression; fear
	Reversed	release of tension and worry; sunshine after storm; Thank the Lord card
10		utterly crushed and defeated by situation; divorce; bankruptcy; forced to start over
	Reversed	having survived the worst that can happen; recovery from disaster; getting back on feet again
PRINCESS		upsetting message; sharp words; forceful communication; person under 25 who is intelligent and outspoken
	Reversed	misunderstanding; angry words; argument; belligerent young person
PRINCE		taking assertive, courageous action; outspoken strong-willed man (25-40)
	Reversed	acting too pushy; conflict with an aggressive troublemaker (25-40)
QUEEN		woman who is no-nonsense, stern, strong-willed, dominating, take charge
	Reversed	vindictive, jealous, petty, unforgiving, demanding woman
KING		lawyer; doctor; good mind; verbal skills; quick wit; perceptive but don't cross him; man over 40
	Reversed	verbal manipulator; uses people; harsh and merciless; ruthless for power

Cups

Cups deal with emotional issues, love, family, friends and all affairs of the heart. They indicate harmony or disharmony in emotional areas. Upright and reversed meanings of the individual Cup cards are given here.

ACE		new beginning of love and emotional rapport; good karma emotionally; new love relationship or friendship
	Reversed	wishing for new relationship and seeing possibility where none exists; false start; delay of new relationship
2		friendship; pleasant rapport; compatibility of emotional temperament; date
	Reversed	loss of friendship; minor disputes; discord in friendship; one of parties breaking off
3		group of friends; family functions; parties; drinking; fun; entertainment; planned pregnancy
	Reversed	excessive drinking, partying, overindulgence, dissipation, alcoholism, accidental pregnancy; promiscuity
4		boredom; missed opportunity; dissatisfaction; apathetic; uninspired
	Reversed	accepting an opportunity; seeing the value of present situation; motivated; ready for new relationship
5		sense of loss; crying over spilled milk; feeling incomplete without someone
	Reversed	appreciation of what is left over after a loss; self reliant and self sufficient
6		past friends; children; karmic ties (good); return of past lover or friend; gift
	Reversed	need to release friends whom you have outgrown; don't let past lover return
7		confusion; fantasy; too many choices; romantic illusions; rose-colored glasses
	Reversed	willing to focus on one thing or person and get realistic; focused creativity and imagination

8	withdrawing self or affections from a relationship; losing interest; backing off; loneliness; leaving stagnated situation to pursue meaningful interests
Reversed	dance-away lover; commitment phobia; fear of intimacy; settling for mediocrity; returning to situation you withdrew from
9	wish card; perfect dream come true; great enjoyment and fulfillment
Reversed	still hoping and waiting for wish to come true but wish delayed or denied; be sure to know what you want before you wish for it
10	mutual love; perfect love and happiness; rapport on all levels; totally in love; sharing
Reversed	one-sided love; areas of incompatibility; disharmony in relationship; arguments between lovers
PRINCESS	child; gay person; love letter or phone call; invitation for a date or party
Reversed	lack of communication from lover or friend; slow period in dating
PRINCE	charming ladies' man who is pleasant, sensitive and emotionally warm; social invitation
Reversed	Don Juan; Romeo; charming but insincere man; uses women; love them and leave them
QUEEN	caring and nurturing woman; mother; good listener; gentle, romantic, sensitive, emotional; good counselor
Reversed	naive and vulnerable; gullible; easily influenced; friendly but superficial; sucker for a sob story
KING	nurturing father; family man; generous and protective; enjoys people work; likes helping people
Reversed	spoils people; overprotective; smothering; won't let go

Wands

Wands is a creative suit, and deals with inspiration, motivation, visionary causes, intuition, and enthusiasm. Upright and reversed meanings of the individual Wand cards are given here.

ACE	new ideas and creativity, beginning of enterprise or invention
Reversed	canceling of new enterprise; false start; idea ahead of its time; delayed start
2	collaboration of ideas; creative partnership; friendship based on common cause or interest; able to communicate ideas well with other party; negotiation
Reversed	creative differences; incompatible values and goals
3	group creativity; fulfillment of creative ideas; invention; making a new idea work; creative flow
Reversed	still some bugs in new enterprise; delays and setbacks; creative block
4	marriage; partnership; establishment of creative goals in workable form
Reversed	living together; dissolving partnership; conflict over creative goals
5	competition; disputes; lawsuit; clash of wills; promotion of business
Reversed	peace after disputes; settlement of lawsuits; cooperation
6	realization of creative dreams at work, arts or sciences; pleasure and victory after hard work
Reversed	disillusionment and defeat of dreams; rewards delayed; opponent wins
7	success against opposition; position of advantage in business; victory through courage
Reversed	feeling threatened; losing ground; show of strength but feels inadequate

8	air travel; good news comes fast; love letters; haste; great hope; approach to a goal
Reversed	delay of travel; news or reaching goal; arrows of jealousy; stagnation of affairs
9	ready for what comes; waiting and watching; be patient; strength in reserve
Reversed	unprepared for problems that may arise; impatient; scattered energies; defensive
10	carrying heavy burden; workaholic; too much pressure and responsibility; abuse of power; all work and no play
Reversed	heavy load lifted; delegates responsibility; able to play and enjoy life now
PRINCESS	young person under 25 who is enthusiastic, enterprising, and creative; good news
Reversed	young person who is flighty, scatterbrained, and over-reactive; bad news
PRINCE	man (25-40) who is energetic, hasty, ardent; spur-of-the-moment person; change of residence; travel; quick departure
Reversed	jealous lover; man who is too pushy, unreliable, inconsistent, impatient
QUEEN	woman who is creative, ardent, enthusiastic, dynamic, enterprising; bubbly personality
Reversed	woman who is flighty, scatterbrained, hysterical under pressure, always late
KING	creative man of vision who isn't afraid to risk and speculate; self-starter; open to new ideas; self-made; entrepreneur
Reversed	man who is impulsive in business decisions; falls for get-rich-quick schemes; con artist/promoter

Pentacles

Pentacles deal with practicality, money, material possessions, and are a work-oriented suit. Upright and reversed meanings of the individual Pentacle cards are given here.

ACE	new financial venture which will be beneficial
Reversed	timing wrong for initiating new venture; false start; delayed start
2	considering two ventures, juggling two work situations; working two jobs
Reversed	alone in business; working one job after juggling two things; settling on one venture; business decisions
3	work which is very fulfilling or best vocation; achievement of expertise
Reversed	over-qualified or bored because nothing new to learn; mediocrity; too critical of self or others
4	financially stable and secure; solid investments; concerned with money and possessions
Reversed	greedy; penny-pinching; grasping and materialistic; stingy; fear of poverty; self-protective
5	unemployed; lay off or getting fired; money very tight; freelance work; uncertain about career
Reversed	going back to work after unemployment; money coming in again; steady work; decision about career
6	good karma regarding money; universe provides; gift; loan; grant of money; benefactor
Reversed	having to repay debts; non-renewal of loan or grant; benefactor stops; support withdrawn
7	unexpected money comes in; job promotion or raise; business travel; good business investment
Reversed	unexpected shake-up in work or in finances; unexpected expense; bad business investment

8	learning a new skill; going to school; training; selling something
Reversed	losing interest in skill; dropping out of school; delay or slow down in sales
9	financially taken care of; buying something; solitary affluence; love of home and gardens; spending money on home, real estate, or office
Reversed	danger of burglary; house expense; financial loss; selling a house; moving an office
10	riches; inheritance; corporate prosperity; family money; a windfall or large sum of money gained
Reversed	corporate losses; heavy money losses; trouble over inheritance; family problems; forced to sell a house or land
PRINCESS	a scholar; good management of money by person under 25; good message about money; contracts; negotiations about money
Reversed	waste of material things; news of loss of money; young person who is self-critical
PRINCE	hard-working, patient, responsible man (25-40); coming or going of money matters
Reversed	man who is dull, unprogressive, workaholic, and overcritical about details
QUEEN	woman who is practical, resourceful in business, well-organized, go-getter
Reversed	superficial, materialistic woman; status seeker; name dropper; wants to look rich; gold-digger
KING	business man of means; merchant or boss; banker; real estate; reliable; math and financial ability
Reversed	poor business sense; wasteful and disorganized; wheeler-dealer

Aces Through Tens

Overview

Learning the meanings of a Minor Arcana card is simplified by blending the meaning of the number of the card with the meanings of its suit.

For example, all **Twos** deal with maintaining balance between two people, situations, or viewpoints. By understanding the general "two" energy and blending the meanings of each suit, we can conclude that the:

- Two of Swords relates to a stalemate because of opposing forces
- Two of Cups involves emotional sharing and friendship
- Two of Wands combines creativity and inspiration through collaboration
- Two of Pentacles pertains to balancing two financial situations.

The same process applies to the other numbers up to 10. All of the **Aces** deal with initiating new beginnings and projects.

The **Threes** relate to blending three elements, people, or situations through synthesis and group energy. The 3 of Swords expresses the jealousy and discord that results when this cooperation is lacking.

The **Fours** involve building and maintaining foundations to insure stability.

The **Fives** describe the need to adapt to the disruptions of unexpected or unwanted changes.

The **Sixes** relate to encouraging progress and help from others as well as a strong connection to ideals.

The **Sevens** pertain to a shift in perspective through insight into a situation. The awareness gained can allow necessary change to occur.

The **Eights** bring power, control, and mastery to a situation and emphasize strength through self-reliance.

The **Nines** signify the culmination of the energy of each suit in its most intense form, bringing completion.

The **Tens** express mastery of the lessons and energy of each suit. They signal renewal through the beginning of a new cycle on a higher turn of the spiral.

Three or Four of a Kind in a Spread

Since there are four Aces through Kings in the deck, at times you will see three or four of the same numbered or Court card in a spread. When this happens, it reinforces the basic meaning of the type of card involved. For example, with three or four Three's, the emphasis is on creativity, synthesis, self-expression, and collaboration.

To summarize:

1 — new beginnings, initiative
2 — relationship, duality, collaboration
3 — synthesis, expression, cooperation
4 — foundation, stability
5 — change, instability, disruption
6 — assistance, idealism, encouragement
7 — unexpected change, perception, awareness
8 — control, power, self-reliance
9 — completion, fulfillment, culmination
10 — renewal, mastery
Princesses — news, communication, thoughts, and children
Princes — coming and going, travel, and quick action
Queens — women or female influence in society
Kings — men or male influence in society

Preponderance of Suits

You may also see spreads where half or more cards are in one suit. On these occasions, you should emphasize the suit's basic meaning in your reading.

Cups — emotional matters, love, and affection
Pentacles — financial and business matters
Swords — courage, will, and potential stress or conflict
Wands — creativity, inspiration, and enterprise

Aces

The Ace of any suit represents the purest form of the energy of the suit. With the Sword suit, the Ace expresses courage and conviction. With Cups, new emotional connections are forged. The Ace of Wands unleashes the inspiration of creativity while the Ace of Pentacles seeks expression in the material world.

THE ACE OF SWORDS
(Courage)

UPRIGHT MEANING: This card shows a regal sword surrounded by a dazzling light. The illumination of a keen intellect can shed a laser beam of light on any situation. As the beginning of the Sword suit, the Ace signifies the force of will and strength to take a stand despite opposing viewpoints. By using the intellect rather than physical force, strong convictions can create positive change without violence. In the martial arts, if a person is centered in their "chi" energy just below the navel, they can divert even the most aggressive attack. The courage and clarity of the Ace of Swords comes from taking a mental stand and backing it up with integrity.

Example Situation: A political canditate announces that he is running for office.

IN A SPREAD: The timing is right for you to assert your will and determination, especially if you have taken a back seat to others' leadership too long. After getting very clear about what you want to manifest in your life, put that idea out into the world with clarity and conviction. The force of your ideas communicated with confidence can let people know what your boundaries are. Those who envy your strong will and conviction may accuse you of too much intensity or force.

Example Situation: A used car salesman in a television commercial promises bargains.

REVERSED MEANING: You are forcing your will on a situation and may encounter opposition. The timing may not be right for stating your case or asserting your ideas. An excess of intensity and willfulness could make you appear pushy. Try to relax and detach from outcomes or delay initating new projects.

THE ACE OF CUPS
(New Friendships)

UPRIGHT MEANING: In the Ace of Cups, a golden grail rests beneath the ocean floor with waterfalls spilling over the brim at the surface. A radiant sun and stars emanate from the glowing pool of water on the surface. These beautiful symbols suggest the the beginning of a relationship of love, empathy, and openness. The water of emotion spilling over in the picture allows light and joy to expand both parties. The opportunity is being offered for both parties to open their hearts to each other. The relationship may be friendship with the **2 of Cups**, a romance with the **Lovers**, **7 of Cups**, or **10 of Cups** or a karmic connection of almost instant rapport with the **6 of Cups**.

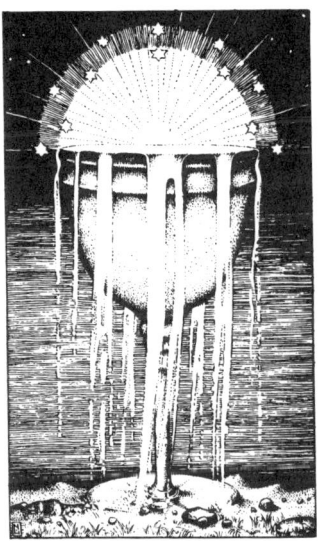

Example Situation: A newly divorced woman attends a singles' function.

IN A SPREAD: You are ready to allow new social contacts into your life and will benefit from parties, groups, and recreational activities. A new person in your life could help you express deeper levels of intimacy than you were able to trust before. A renewal of an existing relationship may occur with the **8 of Cups** R also in the spread. The return of an old lover is possible with the **7 of Swords R**.

Example Situation: A young man writes a love poem after only one dance with a woman.

REVERSED MEANING: Here, a lack of emotional depth can keep relationships on a superficial level. A tendency to be "in love with love" can keep you from really getting to know someone before you give your heart. Avoid the temptation to rush into a relationship or read deeper involvement into what may be a passing acquaintance. This card can also mean a delay in starting a friendship or romance.

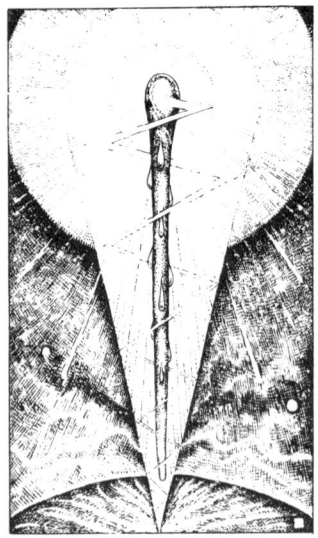

THE ACE OF WANDS
(Creativity)

UPRIGHT MEANING: The Ace of Wands shows a wand springing from the earth surrounded by a bolt of lightning with brilliant golden light radiating from it. This is the wand of creative inspiration and excitement about new enterprises. A new creative idea may be bubbling up with a fiery enthusiasm to make it happen. Often, an urgency or impatience accompanies the energy of the Ace of Wands that needs the grounding of practical execution. The **4 of Pentacles** or the **Emperor** will give stability to the creative vision. The originality of the **Magician** could mean that the idea is marketable as an invention or innovation.

Example Situation: A writer gets an idea for a new book.

IN A SPREAD: An exciting inspiration is ready to grab your imagination. Let your enthusiasm guide you to explore the idea in greater depth. The surrounding cards in the spread will describe the best expression for your idea: Cups relate to inspiration in emotional areas, Wands add extra weight to creative expression, Swords blend inspiration with mental concepts, and Pentacles may help the idea to manifest concretely. Your hobbies may help you give your creative expression free rein.

Example Situation: A hastily written manuscript is rejected by a publisher.

REVERSED MEANING: You may be so caught up in the fervor of your new idea that you are rushing its execution. Your idea may be valuable for your personal awareness but not successful in the marketplace. It may be premature for you to express your idea to others. It may need more time to gestate within your own mind.

THE ACE OF PENTACLES
(New Financial Venture)

UPRIGHT MEANING: A glowing pentacle emerges from the earth. Boulders and crystals surround the Ace of Pentacles in the picture symbolizing the practicality and earthiness of the Pentacle suit. The Pentacle suit also relates to money and financial enterprises and the Ace of Pentacles can indicate new financial ventures and opportunities. The extent of financial gain from the new venture will be determined by the surrounding cards. The **Sun**, **Empress**, or **10 of Pentacles** can mean a very successful venture, while the **4 of Pentacles** or **7 of Pentacles** describe moderate success.

Example Situation: An aspiring entrepreneur opens a franchise.

IN A SPREAD: The timing could be right to launch a new business or financial venture. Money will be well spent at this time to buy office equipment, furniture, and supplies. An idea that has been in the background can now be marketed productively.

Example Situation: A restaurant opens its doors and goes out of business within 6 months.

REVERSED MEANING: A business venture could be risky or premature at this time. Marketing and advertising are inadvisable until market or financial conditions improve. Spending additional money on a business venture may be throwing good money after bad. With the **6 of Wands R**, the **Empress R**, or the **10 of Pentacles R**, a business may be failing.

Twos

The Two of any suit pertains to partnership and duality. With the Sword suit, the relationship creates ambivalence as a stalemate. With Cups, the union is one of friendship and love. The Two of Wands relates to creative collaboration while the Two of Pentacles shows the juggling of two financial situations.

THE TWO OF SWORDS
(Stalemate)

UPRIGHT MEANING: Under the light of the full moon, a woman sits beside a pond with her cat beside her. She gazes into the water below, seemingly unaware of the two swords wedged into the nearby shore. The picture displayed is one of inactivity because the 2 of Swords represents indecision and ambivalence. The cat and the pond show how the instincts and emotions can be comforting when your mind seems to be running in circles. A paradoxical or "catch 22" situation may make it difficult to see a resolution. Another person may have such divergent viewpoints that you lose sight of your own preferences. You may be on hold because of outside circumstances and must wait for others to make their decisions to move forward.

Example Situation: A disciple of zen is stumped by the koan given to him by his teacher.

IN A SPREAD: You are undecided about making a difficult choice. Neither choice feels like a good one and you fear making the "wrong" decision. If you tend to chronically procrastinate about making decisions, look back at the past opportunities you missed by this fear of committment. Sometimes, the worst decision is not to decide. This card with the **Hanged Man** can mean that you may not have much control over this situation and must wait for others to act.

Example Situation: After lengthy deliberation, a chess player makes a crucial move.

REVERSED MEANING: You have overcome your avoidance of a dilemma in your life and reached a decision you can live with. You have also learned that the pain of procrastination and ambivalence was greater than your fear once you exercised your best judgment. With the **Hanged Man R**, outside circumstances may now allow your progress, and with the **Hanged Man R** and **Strength**, a tendency to attract victimizing situations may have been reversed.

THE TWO OF CUPS
(Friendship)

UPRIGHT MEANING: This card portrays Humphrey Bogart and Ingrid Bergman embracing each other in a kiss surrounded by flowers. Two cups stand in front of them radiating shimmering haloes. This card represents the love and affection that can flow between compatible people. It often represents friendship and dating but can indicate intense romantic love with the **Lovers** or the **10 of Cups**. Through the emotional sharing that this card symbolizes, each party is reaching out to another person to express his feelings and need for social contact. The other cards in the spread will indicate how receptive the other person is to a deeper relationship.

Example Situation: A young man asks a young woman to join him for coffee.

IN A SPREAD: The 2 of Cups shows that the goodwill of a friend can help smooth out any situation you are asking about. Social outings or discussing problems with a friend can ease your situation. If you are lonely, making an effort to bring a companion into your life may be timely now. Pleasant dating experiences are likely.

Example Situation: The "odd couple" decide to move in together.

REVERSED MEANING: You have some significant personality differences with a person that are causing disruptions in your relationship. Ignoring irritating but "minor" areas of incompatibility will create greater discord. An open discussion of differing preferences and needs can lead to workable compromises. You may be happier with someone more similar in temperament.

THE TWO OF WANDS
(Collaboration)

UPRIGHT MEANING: A proud and confident man standing in a natural setting between two wands stares into the distance with a visionary look in his eyes. A bright sun and clouds are at his back. He symbolizes a confident outlook about the future and a positive collaboration with another person to actualize the vision. A person who share your values and goals could bring greater inspiration to your creative projects. The shared excitement and enthusiasm as the ideas come into manifestation keep the momentum going. Another person's feedback can give greater objectivity to your considerations. Negotiations could go well when this card accompanies **Justice**, **Judgement**, or Pentacle cards.

Example Situation: A couple excitedly review the blueprint for their new house.

IN A SPREAD: Your creative ideas and goals need feedback from another person of like mind. Ask for a critique from someone whose ideas you value or consider collaborating with someone on the project. Friendly negotiations based on a "Win/Win" approach can fall into place now.

Example Situation: A brilliant screenplay writer gives up editorial approval in the contract for a movie based on her work.

REVERSED MEANING: Your goals may be too short-sighted or be based on superficial values. People who have different values and goals could misdirect your creativity and block your inspiration. Stay connected to the purity of your initial vision for the future. Negotiating with someone who is inflexible and self-serving may be self-defeating.

THE TWO OF PENTACLES
(Balancing Financial Affairs)

UPRIGHT MEANING: A man is maintaining a delicate balance with one foot within each of two pentacles in the sand on a seashore. Rather than sailing off for adventures on the ship behind him, he is coming to shore to accomplish practical, grounded tasks. To his right is a serpent coiled as if to strike signifying the dangers of relying on logic alone. He wears two pentacles inscribed on his shirt and his left hand is placed between his heart and his throat. He looks to his left toward a bird perched on a piling and flowers and foliage below. These symbols suggests that the man will need to access his intuition and emotions to maintain his balance. The 2 of Pentacles relates to two or more sources of income, possibly out of need with the **5 of Pentacles**, or out of a need for variety with the **Magician** or **Fool**. By considering different ways of generating money and expressing your talents, you remain open and flexible about opportunities.

Example Situation; An office worker creates crafts at home and sells them at weekend flea markets.

IN A SPREAD: You are successful at juggling two or more different projects now and enjoy the diversity of different careers. You may be considering many different options for money-making potential. By taking the time to explore a range of possibilities without narrowing them down too quickly, you can choose more wisely how to prioritize.

Example Situation; A backpacker working his way through Europe decides to pursue a degree in college.

REVERSED MEANING: You may feel you are dropping the ball too often in juggling different responsibilities. If you are working more than one job, it may be a good time to consolidate your work. You may feel the need to focus on one project at a time and give greater energy and depth to it.

Threes

The Three of any suit represents synthesis and expression. With the Sword suit, this harmony is lacking, resulting in heartbreak. With Cups, the harmony is cause for celebration. The Three of Wands represents creative flow and self-expression, while the Three of Pentacles stands for mastery.

THE THREE OF SWORDS
(Heartbreak)

UPRIGHT MEANING: Three mourners stand before a grave marked by three swords piercing the rose of affection. Dark clouds gather in the distance. These symbols of intensity and mourning convey the deep emotional suffering and separation connected with this card. Often, the pain is associated with jealousy or envy poisoning a relationship. The constant anger and turmoil has continued for some time and may have brought the relationship to the point of separation. A third party may be creating a triangle situation that is destroying trust in the union. Divorce is likely with the **Tower**, **4 of Wands R**, **10 of Pentacles R**, or **10 of Swords**. With health cards, such as the **Star R**, the **Tower**, or the **8 of Swords**, heart trouble can be indicated.

Example Situation: A woman obsessed with her lover accuses him of infidelity.

IN A SPREAD: The 3 of Swords often relates to a destructive relationship pattern. You may tend to attract partners who clash with you yet bring out obsessive and possessive intensity in you. You may have become "addicted" to dramatic conflicts and passionate reconciliations. If you feel you have been enduring abuse in a relationship, ask yourself what the "hook" is that is keeping you there. This relationship and previous ones may have served to help you remember and resolve childhood abuse. Once these wounds are healed, you will be able to attract more loving and healthy relationships.

Example Situation: A man recovers quickly after divorcing an abusive alcoholic partner.

REVERSED MEANING: You are ready to release an abusive situation without great heartache because you have come to the verge of separation repeatedly in the past. Your possessiveness or resentment over infidelity can pass quickly from your life if you do not hold on to it.

THE THREE OF CUPS
(Celebration)

UPRIGHT MEANING: A man and woman raise their arms in celebration as three cups before them overflow with the water of emotion. The 3 of Cups symbolizes a comfortable conviviality with other people at gatherings for fun and celebration. Parties, bars, and sports events are places where people relax and enjoy each other's company. Weddings, baptisms, traditional holidays, and family reunions also bring families closer together for joy and renewal. This card often symbolizes three people who are especially close to each other and get together regularly. The 3 of Cups with the **Empress** or **Page of Cups** can show a planned conception and birth.

Example Situation: Co-workers meet regularly for "happy hour" after work.

IN A SPREAD: You would benefit by attending a party, wedding, or other social gathering. The sense of camaraderie that groups can offer may encourage you to let your hair down. Don't be afraid to indulge your inner child with some creative "silliness", such as party games or practical jokes.

Example Situation: An unhappy woman drinks heavily in bars and behaves promiscuously.

REVERSED MEANING: This card can mean that the fun of parties, celebrating, and drinking has degenerated into self-indulgence and dissipation. Drinking, smoking, and unhealthy eating habits may be excessive. With the **Moon** or **7 of Cups**, drinking, smoking, and drug use could create serious problems with addiction. Look at the underlying issues behind your desire to escape into excesses. With the **Empress R**, **Moon**, or **7 of Cups**, sexual carelessness can put you at risk for venereal disease, AIDS, or unwanted pregnancies.

THE THREE OF WANDS
(Creative Flow)

UPRIGHT MEANING: A woman swaying in meditation raises her arms to the sun above. Three wands springing from the earth surround her and on the ground in front of her are three lotuses representing the opening of the crown chakra to receive cosmic inspiration. The picture on this card evokes the receptivity to creative flow that the 3 of Wands symbolizes. By opening ourselves up to input from our Higher Power and the vision of others, we allow greater creativity to flow through us. The fulfillment of creative goals by making a new idea work is often indicated by this card. Consultants, freelance writers, and artists often pool creative ideas for mutual benefit. By joining with others in a group venture, goals that might be delayed can often be realized much sooner.

Example Situation: After a vivid dream about a new screenplay, a writer has dinner with two creative friends to brainstorm about the idea.

IN A SPREAD: You can get valuable feedback and share the creative perspective of others by taking a class in your area of interest. Your creative ideas could be given new direction by forming a team of three or more participants who critique each other's work and offer suggestions. Your ideas need exposure to others so that you can fine-tune the details before finalizing a product.

Example Situation: At a corporate staff meeting, an aspiring writer shows the group an outline for a book he wants to write about palmistry.

REVERSED MEANING: Your creativity may feel blocked and disconnected from the "Muse" of inspiration. The timing may not be right for pressing forward with your project. You may be "casting your pearls before swine" if people around you are unreceptive to your vision. Withdraw from those who do not resonate to your creative goals and ask for appropriate feedback from your dreams and intuitions.

THE THREE OF PENTACLES
(Mastery)

UPRIGHT MEANING: Three workman are busily constructing a stone building where three pentacles are inset forming a huge window. The 3 of Pentacles represents a mastery and expertise derived from many years of training and practice. With the **Hermit**, people may look to you for expert guidance or ask you to be a teacher or consultant in your chosen field. With the **Magician** or **Star**, you may be a "natural" at your chosen field and develop mastery in a short time. Even though this card means mastery, it also implies a continuing desire to improve skills and expand knowledge. This card can mean perfectionism and discrimination about life in general, indicating that you will look for high quality in any purchases you make.

Example Situation: A golf pro shoots a hole-in-one.

IN A SPREAD: You have reached a high level of achievement in an area of your life. The surrounding cards will describe in what arena your mastery lies. Possibly, a hobby you excel at could become a source of extra income. With Cups or the **Lovers** prominent, you tend to choose friends or lovers who meet your need for high standards.

Example Situation: An expert carpenter cuts corners on materials and workmanship on a tract house project.

REVERSED MEANING: You may be frustrated with the lack of creative challenge in a current situation. Even if you are over-qualified and the work is routine, abide by your high standards rather than produce lackluster work. With a skill you are still striving to master, this card can mean you may be tempted to settle for mediocrity. With Cups in the spread, you may be over-critical of others, especially in love or friendship,

Fours

The Four of any suit represents foundation, stability, and the status quo. With the Sword suit, the status quo is being preserved during a period of recuperation. With Cups, the status quo is the result of apathy. The Four of Wands represents the stability of a business or marriage partnership, while the Four of Pentacles stands for financial security.

THE FOUR OF SWORDS
(Recuperation)

UPRIGHT MEANING: This card shows four men resting at an oasis in a desert. They have laid down their four swords on a rug decorated with the symbol for Jupiter in a background of stars. The oasis is a fitting symbol for the rest and recuperation that this card is concerned with. The protection of Jupiter allows these travelers to lay down their arms and relax without fear of conflict. Similarly, the 4 of Swords allows a time for you to be inactive and heal from a period of mental, emotional, or physical stress. With the **Star R**, **Strength R**, the **8 of Swords**, or the **Tower**, a health crisis may arise requiring hospitalization. By itself, the 4 of Swords often refers to a quiet period of inactivity and rest. With travel cards, it can relate to a vacation to a restful location.

Example Situation: After a major move, a couple spends a week at a cabin in the woods.

IN A SPREAD: You may need to take a break from a life that has become frenetic. You may be experiencing minor headaches or sore throats letting you know that you are overtaxed and need rest. If you tend to overdo in your work, this card can be a warning to bring balance back into your life. If you ignore the need for more rest, a cold or flu may force you to slow down. Try spending an entire day reading on the couch, sipping soothing hot tea, and relaxing in a hot bath.

Example Situation: A man returns to work after a bout with the flu.

REVERSED MEANING: It is time to resume the normal tempo of your activities after a period of rest and recuperation. If you have been ill, this card can indicate full recovery, especially if the **Star**, **Strength**, or the **Sun** are also present.

THE FOUR OF CUPS
(Apathy)

UPRIGHT MEANING: This card shows a young man seated on a picnic blanket. He seems lost in thought and unaware of the beautiful surroundings around him and the four cups and four lotuses close by. This can be a card of dissatisfaction and apathy regarding the bounty you already have and a warning not to overlook opportunities for joy in your everyday life. Because all of the four's relate to stability and the status quo, they do not usually relate to excitement or adventure. With the 4 of Cups, there is a tendency for you to underrate the contentment of your life and take things for granted.

Example Situation: A housewife with a loving family and comfortable home shops to stifle her boredom.

IN A SPREAD: You may be tempted to upset the stability of a good life you have developed out of a sense of boredom. Instead, seek areas of your life that spark your interest for future development. If nothing seems appealing to you, know that this phase of dissatisfaction will pass and new interests will dissipate the apathy you feel now.

Example Situation; After dating several men half-heartedly, a woman feels passionately drawn to a new man.

REVERSED MEANING: Here, the "ho-hum" attitude toward life has passed and you are ready to plunge into new relationships and launch new projects. You can see the opportunities for enjoyment in even the small everyday events of your life.

THE FOUR OF WANDS
(Partnership)

UPRIGHT MEANING: A ballet dancer leans forward in a graceful movement with one arm and leg extended behind her. She dances within a spiral formed by four upright wands and four flowers. In the distance are pyramids and a white dove flying overhead, symbolizing symmetry and harmony. The beauty of these symbols reflects the grounding of the Wand suit in manifestation as a partnership. Traditionally, this card was the marriage card and with the **Lovers**, **3 of Cups**, **9 of Cups**, or **10 of Cups**, can signify a marriage. Because of the stability of the four energy, the idealism, creativity, and inspiration of the Wand suit is now ready for grounding in committed partnerships. With Pentacles, the union can be a solid business partnership or with other Wands, it can be creative collaboration on a concrete goal.

Example Situation: A massage therapist and a chiropractor join forces to open a clinic.

IN A SPREAD: Your vision is ready to be grounded in a concrete, stable expression. A partner may offer the missing elements you have felt were lacking before the idea could come into form. With other favorable cards in the spread, you benefit now more from partnership than from going it alone.

Example Situation: A couple move in together and discover that their different habits and lifestyles make commitment unlikely.

REVERSED MEANING: You may feel uncertain that your partner shares your direction in life and question your commitment to the relationship. With the **3 of Swords**, **10 of Cups R**, or the **Tower**, you may want to dissolve the marriage or partnership after enduring repeated upsets. You may encounter conflicts in a shaky business partnership about decision-making or handling money. With favorable cards, this card can indicate living together rather than the formality of marriage.

THE FOUR OF PENTACLES
(Security)

UPRIGHT MEANING: A businessman in an office faces a woman who may be interviewing for a job or acting as his assistant. On the wall behind him are four pentacles and the sign Capricorn. The practicality and need for security of the 4 of Pentacles are well reflected in these symbols. This card relates to the security of knowing you have enough basic "bread and butter" money in your life to cover your basic needs without worry. It can refer to a fairly routine job with moderate pay but good benefits. The 4 of Pentacles can show a conservative streak in terms of both financial investments and emotional risks. You may be looking for a "sure thing" in both areas without any unexpected surprises. You prefer to build slowly and solidly for the future without having to rely upon others either financially or emotionally.

Example Situation: An office worker saves money from each paycheck and has a regular Saturday night date with his girlfriend.

IN A SPREAD: You feel secure and self-reliant about your financial stability. Your love of planning and predictability can dampen the spontaneity of social events or travel. By seeking out only safe experiences and relationships, you may be sacrificing both the growth and the excitement that stretching your horizons can bring.

Example Situation: A wealthy miser hoards his money and fears that he is on the brink of poverty.

REVERSED MEANING: You may be experiencing strong fears and insecurities about lack of money in your life. Whether or not this is literally true, you may find it difficult to trust other people financially or emotionally. With the **Devil**, the **Moon**, or the **9 of Swords**, possessiveness, greed, and obsessiveness about money can be symptoms of previous traumas surfacing. Giving generously to yourself and others can help to heal your childhood scars from lack of love or money.

Fives

The Five of any suit represents change and instability. With the Sword suit, the instability is caused by betrayal. With Cups, the feeling is one of regret. The Five of Wands represents competition, while the Five of Pentacles stands for insecurity.

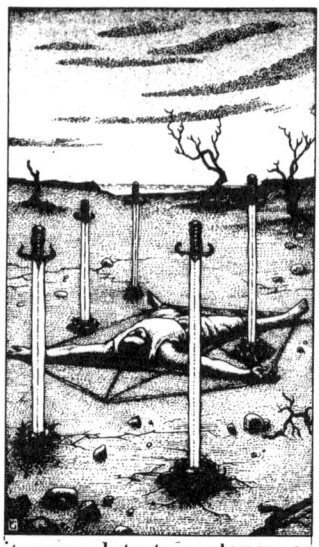

THE FIVE OF SWORDS
(Betrayal)

UPRIGHT MEANING: This card shows a man in a desert environment lying on his back within a pentacle inscribed on the ground. The pentacle in magical literature symbolized humanity with its five senses and upright stature. Five swords signifying betrayal pierce the roses of affection that surround him. This card reflects the prostration and grief felt after being sabotaged by someone you have trusted. The hidden enemy in your close associations can create devastating pain and shock when revealed. With the **3 of Swords**, it can relate to jealousy or an unfaithful lover and with the **Princess of Swords R**, it may warn of spiteful gossip or slander. This card can also relate to unresolved resentment from prior betrayals when combined with the **5 of Cups** or the **6 of Cups**.

Example Situation: A woman's friend at work sabotages her promotion by spreading gossip about her personal life.

IN A SPREAD: You should be careful to look for the hidden agendas of those close to you. Your best interests may be playing second fiddle to a friend's ambitions or manipulations. Trust your instincts if you sense something amiss and confront the situation. An old enemy may resurface and attempt to set the stage for new treachery. If so, this can be an opportunity for you not to be taken in by the deception and emerge unscathed.

Example Situation: After an opponent launches a vicious mud-slinging campaign, the victor clears his reputation and emerges the winner.

REVERSED MEANING: You are in a position to vindicate yourself of any gossip or acts of betrayal. Your enemy will be exposed as spiteful and malicious and you will suffer no harm from the attack. With the **Moon** or **9 of Swords**, you may need to release resentments over past betrayals.

THE FIVE OF CUPS
(Regret)

UPRIGHT MEANING: This card depicts a woman with her head bowed in grief seated at a table where five cups have overturned spilling their emotional contents. A dried rose signifying a lost love rests on the table in front of her. This card symbolizes "crying over spilled milk" and vain regrets for past actions. Often, it is difficult to let go of the past because of obsessive preoccupation with what might have been. The tendency is for you to blame yourself for the emotional loss rather than see the other person's part objectively. With the **Sun R**, **9 of Swords**, or **10 of Swords**, the grief may be causing deep depression.

Example Situation: After her son runs away from home, a woman suffers constant regret over the argument that separated them.

IN A SPREAD: Let go of your regret and have compassion for where you were in your life when the regrettable incident occurred. Accept the fact that your present wisdom was gained from learning from past mistakes. If necessary, make amends to the other person so that you can forgive yourself. If you continue to blame the other person, ask for insight and compassion about the other person's perspective.

Example Situation: A man is finally able to accept a painful divorce and appreciate the opportunity for happier relationships.

REVERSED MEANING: You have processed your regrets and are ready to accept that life often teaches through emotional pain. You can return the cups of your life to an upright position and fill them with new emotional connections and growth.

THE FIVE OF WANDS
(Competition)

UPRIGHT MEANING: Two men lunge at each other using five wands as weapons. This card symbolizes friendly competition in the sense of sports or business rivalry when it appears with other Wands or Pentacles. It can show a need to be assertive in efforts to promote a business or an idea. With positive Pentacles, it might be a good time to launch an advertising campaign. With cards of conflict such as the **3 of Swords**, **5 of Swords**, or **7 of Swords**, it can indicate anger and violence. The **Chariot R** or the **Magician R** can show a ruthless person who is out of control and could be dangerous.

Example Situation: A drug store mails out a coupon booklet to stimulate business.

IN A SPREAD: You may be feeling competitive and challenging energy coming from another person. If you sense that hostility or anger is being triggered in a situation, examine your own motives and deeper feelings before confronting the situation. In a business or creative venture, consider how you can "beat the bushes" for greater revenue or exposure.

Example Situation: After living in a big city ghetto, a young man moves to a small town of 250 residents.

REVERSED MEANING: The anger and hostility you have felt has passed and you feel you can relax your guard now. You can afford to enjoy the peace in the present without waiting for the other shoe to drop. In business, previous promotional activities can now produce additional revenue.

THE FIVE OF PENTACLES
(Insecurity)

UPRIGHT MEANING: In the rubble of a decaying city, refugees struggle to survive. This card graphically depicts the fear and alienation that accompanies unemployment and poverty. It also represents financial insecurity as a result of freelance or commission work without a predictable paycheck to count on. Although it usually relates to financial insecurity, this card can also reflect poverty consciousness and alienation, even when money is abundant. With the **8 of Cups** or the **Hermit R**, the 5 of Pentacles can describe a period when a person feels lonely, abandoned, and out in the cold emotionally.

Example Situation: An unemployed woman is evicted from her apartment and becomes homeless.

IN A SPREAD: You may be feeling fear about your ability to survive financially. If you are not unemployed, the nature of your work may provoke these insecurities from time to time. If your work is seasonal or the money highly unpredictable, consider a savings account or line of credit to take the sting out of temporary shortages. If money is not the cause of the insecurity, explore reasons that you may feel needy and cut off from others. With the **3 of Pentacles** or **8 of Pentacles**, you could be working to help the plight of the needy.

Example Situation: A long-term employee, shattered by the closing of a local plant, finds freelance work by using his skills as a consultant.

REVERSED MEANING: A period of unemployment or financial uncertainty has ended and you can breathe easy. Your freelance or seasonal work may increase. In your personal life, you feel more accepted and secure.

Sixes

The Six of any suit represents assistance, idealism, and perfection. With the Sword suit, a change for the better comes through assistance. With Cups, the feeling is one of pleasant memories from the past. The Six of Wands represents triumph, while the Six of Pentacles stands for financial aid.

THE SIX OF SWORDS
(Assistance)

UPRIGHT MEANING: A dancer assumes a graceful ballet pose with his toe positioned at the center where the points of six swords come together. Behind him is a staff bearing the caduceus, the symbol of healing. The poise displayed by the dancer signifies that he is able to maintain his center in the midst of difficulties. A healing is taking place in his life and he is headed out of troubled waters. He may be receiving counseling and heeding good advice about avoiding further problems. A trip over water or near water is also a traditional meaning for this card.

Example Situation: A substance abuser starts attending AA meetings.

IN A SPREAD: You are now headed in a direction that will help you heal from a difficult period in your life. By integrating the insights you are getting and the advice you are receiving into your daily life, you will be able to navigate the remaining passage toward wholeness. Alternative healing techniques such as massage, body work, flower essences, or oriental medicine may speed the process. A trip or outing near water can help you with your emotional cleansing.

Example Situation: A battered woman returns to the abusing relationship.

REVERSED MEANING: You are being drawn back into debilitating situations that will create further problems. If the **Devil**, **Moon**, or **7 of Cups** also appear in the spread, you may be tempted to escape into addictive behaviors again. You may be entrenched in denial and refuse to listen to good advice at this time. Ask for guidance before panicking and backsliding into destructive behavior.

THE SIX OF CUPS
(The Past)

UPRIGHT MEANING: A young man plants a platonic kiss on the cheek of a young woman as the dove of gentle love flies overhead. Six cups rise from the reeds at their feet. The 6 of Cups represents the nostalgia of childhood memories and those ties that feel as close as family to us. Karmic connections with immediate rapport and positive bonds with children also relate to this card. You may receive good karma in the form of gifts if the **Empress** or the **6 of Pentacles** also appear in the spread. The return of a karmic lover can be indicated with the **8 of Cups R** or the **7 of Swords R**.

Example Situation: Old college friends reminisce about their escapades.

IN A SPREAD: You may have been reminiscing about pleasant memories shared with loved ones recently. Reconnecting with those you feel kinship with could help you draw sustenance from the past to fuel the future. With the **Princess of Cups**, you may be drawn to spend more time around children.

Example Situation: A woman looks through her childhood photo albums each evening instead of accepting social invitations in her new location.

REVERSED MEANING: You are holding on to the past at the expense of building a future for yourself. With the **7 of Cups** or the **Moon**, it is likely that you are glamourizing the past by overlooking the problems and imperfections that were also present. Accept the reality that things are never the same even if you could go back to the past that you are idealizing. With the **5 of Cups** or the **Lovers R**, you may be obsessing about a lost love and blocking the entry of new romances into your life.

THE SIX OF WANDS
(Triumph)

UPRIGHT MEANING: A man wearing the symbol for Jupiter on his chest and a wreath on his head holds a wand in a triumphant stance. A lion with a crown on its head symbolizing the sign Leo sits in the background. This card symbolizes the triumphant accomplishment of cherished goals. Recognition and achievement in business, arts, or sciences are likely, and with the **Magician**, originality may be richly rewarded. By your persistance in bringing creativity into manifestation, your ideas have received enthusiastic approval.

Example Situation: An artist receives critical acclaim after a one-man show at a prestigious gallery.

IN A SPREAD: When this card appears in a spread, you are encouraged to continue seeking recognition for you are likely to succeed. If difficult cards are nearby, you will overcome obstacles or may have fears about success to process. With the **Sun**, **Empress**, **6 of Pentacles**, or the **10 of Pentacles**, your success may be resounding.

Example Situation: After several interviews with the same employer, a job applicant learns that he has not been chosen for the job.

REVERSED MEANING: You may feel disillusioned and defeated after failing to achieve a cherished goal. Try to see that other options may ultimately be better for your progress. With **Justice R** or **Judgement R**, you may be disappointed in a legal decision. With **Strength R** or the **Star R**, you may be feeling discouraged when in reality, persistence may still lead you to success.

THE SIX OF PENTACLES
(Financial Aid)

UPRIGHT MEANING: A man standing on a pinnacle under a crescent moon extends his arms exuberantly with six pentacles overhead, symbolizing sharing generously. This card relates to the bounty that the Universe can shower on us through benefactors, loans, grants, gifts, or settlements. The kind of money represented by this card is not wages but "found money" or extra money above and beyond our ordinary living expenses. With the **Wheel of Fortune**, the **Empress**, or the **Sun**, the money may come unexpectedly from a game of chance or lucky break. With the **5 of Pentacles**, this card can indicate unemployment compensation or other entitlements.

Example Situation: An impoverished but talented high school student is notified that she had received a scholarship for college study.

IN A SPREAD: You are in a position to receive help and financial assistance from others. Research different sources for the money you need to pursue your dreams. Apply for loans, grants, scholarships, and fellowships for schooling or look for backers or investors if you need capital for business. Good karma in the form of money can be yours for the asking.

Example Situation: A newly graduated dentist pays back his college loans.

REVERSED MEANING: It is time to pay back debts or loans after having received financial assistance from family, schools, banks, or the government. Paying your debts balances your checkbook with the Universe and reaffirms your belief that you will be provided for in the future. Donating to your church or other charities is another way of showing gratitude and giving back. With the **5 of Pentacles**, a loan, grant, or entitlement may not be renewed.

Sevens

The Seven of any suit represents unexpected change, perception, and insight. With the Sword suit, the atmosphere is one of mistrust. With Cups, the insight takes place in the imagination. The Seven of Wands represents a position of advantage, while the Seven of Pentacles stands for a new business perspective.

THE SEVEN OF SWORDS
(Mistrust)

UPRIGHT MEANING: A woman wearing a cape uses it to disguise her actions as she walks amidst seven swords toward a full moon. The eerie landscape on the card conveys the need for watchfulness in the face of possible deception. Traditionally, this is the card of dishonesty and trickery. Being told partial truths or downright lies creates unsettling feelings. The "rip off" can range from insincerity with the **Prince of Cups R** to deliberate theft with the **5 of Swords** or **Moon R**. Victimization by con artists or get-rich-quick scams are also likely with the **Fool R**, **Magician R**, or the **Wheel of Fortune R**. The unfaithfulness of a lover is possible with the **3 of Swords** or **5 of Swords**.

Example Situation: A woman returns home to find her house burglarized.

IN A SPREAD: Pay attention to any misgivings you feel now because you could be victimized by an unscrupulous person. Do not be seduced by hearing what you want to hear or an offer that is "too good to be true." If this card is surrounded by positive cards, you may be defensive and untrusting in your general attitude toward people.

Example Situation: A teenager convicted of petty theft is ordered to make restitution to those he has harmed.

REVERSED MEANING: This card can mean a reversal of the victimizing situation through the return of stolen property or the humble apology of the deceptive person. You will triumph over the "rip off" you have experienced and recover from your victimized feelings.

THE SEVEN OF CUPS
(Imagination)

UPRIGHT MEANING: Seven cups on this card hold a confusing mixture of images. They range from a crown to a snake portraying this card's connection with fantasy and illusion. A man tormented by the crush of agonizing confusion falls prostrate in despair. Usually, being drawn emotionally toward too many choices is creating ambivalence and escapist tendencies. The tendency may be to retreat into fantasy, television watching, or, with many Cups, romantic illusions. Escape into addictions can be indicated by the **Moon, 3 of Cups R**, or **Temperance R** also in the spread. Creative talent and use of the imagination is likely with the **Star** or **Magician**.

Example Situation: A blocked writer spends her days watching "Lifestyles of the Rich and Famous" and soap operas on television.

IN A SPREAD: You may feel overwhelmed by shifting desires and interests. Sleeping too much or escapist activities will only delay your necessary return to realistic goal setting. Make a list of all the attractive possibilities you could choose and prioritize them by preference. Stay focused on the top two or three until you feel some momentum return to your life.

Example Situation: A floundering artist immerses himself in a new line of jewelry that captures his imagination.

REVERSED MEANING: You no longer feel bogged down by confusion and lack of focus and have set realistic goals. You are channeling your imagination into viable projects. The use of creative visualization and meditation can expand your inspiration and attract greater opportunities to you.

THE SEVEN OF WANDS
(Position of Advantage)

UPRIGHT MEANING: A man confidently holds a wand upright in a valiant attempt to ward off attacks from six wands around him. This card relates to the ability to triumph over difficult odds through persistence and courage. In business and other competitive situations, it shows a position of advantage and the opportunity for success. With difficult cards, this card is an encouragement to persist against difficult odds because the tide could turn in your favor at any time. With the **2 of Wands**, your attempts at negotiation could be successful.

Example Situation: During a trial, a defense attorney successfully fends off an attack from the prosecuting attorney.

IN A SPREAD: With the **Hanged Man** or **Strength R**, you may feel exhausted from a continuing battle in your life but should not give up. It is likely that through your valour, you will overcome the opposition and win out. With the **Sun** or **6 of Wands**, triumph is almost certainly assured if you persist.

Example Situation: A woman realizes that she cannot singlehandedly save her failing marriage and seeks a divorce.

REVERSED MEANING: You may be feeling vulnerable and fearful about maintaining a tenuous position. If other cards are positive, these doubts may be unfounded. With difficult cards, you may indeed be fighting a losing battle and would do well to withdraw.

THE SEVEN OF PENTACLES
(New Business Perspective)

UPRIGHT MEANING: A man carries two pentacles as he walks through a desolate terrain where he sees buried and damaged pentacles. The feeling here is one of discouragement and fatigue but only because much effort has been expended and it is time to reevaluate business goals. Without new creative goals and fresh ideas, the business will become barren like the landscape on this card. An unexpected change involving business may occur such as a raise, promotion, business travel, or lucrative investments.

Example Situation: A successful printing company expands to offer their customers rental computer equipment.

IN A SPREAD: It may be time for you to reevaluate your business and financial progress with an eye to integrating the latest technology or information into your work. Be objective about the strategies that have paid off and phase out those that haven't. Don't be afraid to make some bold moves in your future business plans.

Example Situation: A woman suffers major losses when her stocks fall and sales are down at her retail store.

REVERSED MEANING: You could suffer from bad investments or business losses at this time, which could be severe with the **Tower** or **10 of Pentacles R**. Overlooked errors and unexpected expenses are likely to create chaos in your finances. Unexpected turbulence at work may shake up your sense of security there. With Cups, you may not have enough objectivity about emotional areas of your life and may need outside feedback.

Eights

The Eight of any suit represents control, power, and organization. With the Sword suit, restrictive conditions interfere with the exercise of control or power. With Cups, the client withdraws emotionally from a worsening situation. The Eight of Wands represents swiftness in all kinds of messages, while the Eight of Pentacles stands for control and power through education.

THE EIGHT OF SWORDS
(Restriction)

UPRIGHT MEANING: A man and woman pace in a small area bordered by eight swords within prison walls. Dark foreboding clouds loom overhead. This card relates to restriction and inhibition based upon fear of breaking free. Although the obstacles may be external, such as a health problem, more often the prison is created by the mind of the prisoner. The fear of confronting and changing the situation is blocking the normal reaction of casting aside the limiting chains. Because of the severe frustration connected with choosing to stay in a repressive situation, the health may suffer, especially if the **Star R** or **Strength R** are also in the spread. Violent angry outbursts can erupt with the **Chariot R** or the **Ace of Swords R**.

Example Situation: A desperately unhappy man stays with a jealous and controlling wife out of insecurity and fear.

IN A SPREAD: A deep psychological fear is most likely at the root of the severe discomfort you are feeling currently. You may feel so paralyzed at the thought of breaking free that it is best to accept your fear and ask for insight into its deeper cause. Counseling or asking for objective feedback from friends could be helpful. Notice whether astrological timing or the timing of the spread offers a clue as to when the dilemma could be resolved.

Example Situation: After years of abuse, a sexually harrassed woman quits her job and sues her former boss.

REVERSED MEANING: You have faced your fears and realize that you cannot tolerate the limiting conditions of the past. You are now empowered to set boundaries and, if they are not respected, withdraw from your previous prison. You may feel a rush of buried anger and resentment aimed at both your abuser and yourself that needs forgiveness. Your freedom and independence have been hard won and will be richly enjoyed.

THE EIGHT OF CUPS
(Withdrawal)

UPRIGHT MEANING: A man sits downcast in a desolate setting, surrounded by eight empty cups, some strewn at his feet amidst rubble. These symbols relate to emotional indifference and withdrawal of affection from a relationship. The parties may have pulled away from each other emotionally and have felt lonely even within the relationship for some time. A separation is possible without the pain and intensity of the **3 of Swords** because much of the disillusionment with the partnership has already been processed. This card can relate to a sense of personal loneliness and emotional withdrawal from deep connection with other people.

Example Situation: A woman backs off from her lover and spends more and more time with friends and groups.

IN A SPREAD: You have felt the closeness between you and another person diminish over a period of time. The withdrawal of your feelings may be temporary with the **Hermit**, the **4 of Swords**, or the **4 of Cups** and show a need for space in your life to reevaluate your feelings. If you feel drawn in a new direction, it may be time to withdraw gracefully from an emotional connection without a great sense of loss.

Example Situation: After a stale period in their relationship, a couple share new areas of openness and renew their feelings for each other.

REVERSED MEANING: After time to think, you may find that you want to invest more of your emotional energy in a relationship you thought was waning. If this is the case, explore fresh areas for growth and improvement in the relationship instead of settling for the status quo. You may have a pattern of withdrawing when the intimacy deepens, if the **Prince of Cups R** or **Princess of Cups R** also appear in the spread.

THE EIGHT OF WANDS
(Swiftness)

UPRIGHT MEANING: This card shows a man jumping with eight rods flying through the air with great speed. This card is associated with quickness, air travel with travel cards, and good messages of all kinds wiith princesses also in the spread. In business, it pertains to activity picking up and becoming almost frenetic in its pace. Advertising may create many orders and phone calls from customers. In personal matters, it often relates to the rapid involvement of new lovers and to the "arrows of love" coming from love letters, phone messages, or flower deliveries. It also relates to a speedy change of circumstances that is encouraging for achieving cherished hopes.

Example Situation: A saleswoman's voice mailbox is full of messages from new customers wanting to place orders.

IN A SPREAD: With other Wands or Pentacles, you can benefit from an expansive period when the demands for your talents are stepped up. Try to stay organized and relaxed even though your life feels as if it is fast-paced and exciting. With Cups, you may be in great demand socially and be hotly pursued by a new admirer.

Example Situation: A man feels beleagured by delays, mixed messages, and petty annoyances.

REVERSED MEANING: Delays, hassles, and petty jealousy can create considerable irritation for you now. Check for mistakes carefully before submitting work or signing contracts. Your energy may feel jangley and communication with others may be abrupt. Concentrate on projects where you can work alone until the energy shifts.

THE EIGHT OF PENTACLES
(Education)

UPRIGHT MEANING: This card shows a woman holding a bouquet of eight pentacles surrounding a center rose. A ray of awareness descends from above to rest on the bouquet symbolizing the expansion of the mind available through education. This card pertains to the discipline necessary to undergo training in a new skill and to gradually fine tune the ability until the student is proficient at it. It is the card of the apprentice who focuses on the detail and precision of his tasks and takes pride in gradual improvement. It does not refer to mastery because it implies an ongoing learning process in order to integrate new information. With other Pentacles, additional training at work or vocational training can bring financial rewards.

Example Situation: A maintenance worker enrolls in computer programmer training.

IN A SPREAD: Notice which suit predominates in the spread. With Cups, relationship skills could improve through counseling or tools such as self-help books or workshops. With Wands, you could expand your marketing or promotional skills. With Swords, taking a class about an area of assertiveness training, legalities, or abstract concepts could be productive.

Example Situation: A burned-out medical student decides to drop out of medical school.

REVERSED MEANING: You may feel discouraged about an new area of study and worry that you will never be more than mediocre at it. Before dropping out of training that you have invested heavily in, consider whether you are being overly perfectionistic and hard on yourself. If you are feeling bored and unchallenged in an area where you are already skilled, explore a new interest that is appealing.

Nines

The Nine of any suit represents completion and fulfillment. With Swords, the atmosphere is one of worry over the outcome. With Cups, a wish has been fulfilled. The Nine of Wands represents a watch and wait situation, while the Nine of Pentacles stands for a comfortable home.

THE NINE OF SWORDS
(Intense Anxiety)

UPRIGHT MEANING: A terrified man is being struck down by nine swords flying through space at him. A serpent representing repressed fears has been impaled on a sword and buildings are crumbling in the background. These images describe the intensity of the apprehension and dread associated with this card. Because this is a high sword card, it refects a stressful situation that has built to a high pitch of anxiety over time. The problem preys on your mind and may disturb your sleep with insomnia and nightmares. The dominant suit will give clues to the source of the stress. The constant worry may stem from a mental disorder such as depression or paranoia, if the **Moon, Star R**, or **Hanged Man** are also in the spread. Physical breakdown can be indicated with other health cards.

Example Situation: A man who has fallen into deep debt agonizes about how to pay his bills.

IN A SPREAD: You may feel as if you are experiencing the "Dark Night of the Soul" at times. You could be stewing about the difficulties you are undergoing but finding solutions elusive. Counseling, meditation, and stress reduction can help you put things into perspective now. Look back at other stressful situations you have lived through and acknowledge your ability to emerge a survivor from such experiences. An astrological or numerological consultation may help you see that this cycle too shall pass.

Example Situation: A woman who feels suicidal after a divorce sees hope for the future through her love for her daughter.

REVERSED MEANING: You are emerging from a dark tunnel of despair and can now see that hope and optimism lie ahead. This is the "Thank the Lord" card indicating that a long period of anxiety and fear has passed. You can heave a sigh of relief and acknowledge your courage at facing and enduring a difficult passage in your life.

THE NINE OF CUPS
(Wish Fulfillment)

UPRIGHT MEANING: A bright sun and nine golden cups surround a couple who gaze with happiness into each other's eyes. This is the traditional "wish card" and indicates emotional happiness because a cherished dream has been fulfilled. The degree of joy experienced will depend on whether the desire was an outworn wish from earlier times or one consistent with your present life. The surrounding cards will describe your long-term reaction to this wish fulfillment. With the **Empress**, **Wheel of Fortune**, **Magician**, or the **10 of Pentacles**, synchronicity and magical circumstances may bring your cherished wish to you.

Example Situation: A couple takes the trip to Hawaii they have always dreamed of sharing.

IN A SPREAD: You have focused on a desire or wish for some time and are now in a position to see it fulfilled. The initial euphoria can be followed by a letdown if you still feel dissatisfied after manifesting your wish. Notice the Major Arcana cards in the spread for clues about your lessons regarding external happiness versus inner joy.

Example Situation: A woman is frustrated because the contract falls through each time she attempts to buy a house.

REVERSED: Your wish may be denied because you are asking for the impossible or are unconsciously ambivalent about having your dream come true. Picture yourself living the dream you want and see if it feels right for your path in life. Delays caused by outside circumstances can be overcome when timing shifts to your advantage.

THE NINE OF WANDS
(Watch and Wait)

UPRIGHT MEANING: A man stands strong with nine wands around him for his protection. A cobra on one of the wands and the male lion behind him signify the fierce courage he has at his disposal. This card symbolizes the strength held in reserve that comes from previous experience. Although ready for whatever may arise, you realize that the best strategy will evolve by waiting patiently for the next step to reveal itself. Rather than acting impulsively or defensively, you have learned that calm certainty creates the best decisions and is your best defense from attack.

Example Situation: After his company is bought out by a large corporation, an executive continues with his duties until decisions are made about his position.

IN A SPREAD: By waiting and watching the progress of events, you will make greater headway than by pushing your desires forward at this time. You are well prepared for any situations that may arise and do not need to feel defensive. Take your time in making final judgements even though others may be panicking about potential changes.

Example Situation: A woman hears a rumor that her company may lay off some employees and rushes to find another job.

REVERSED MEANING: You may feel vulnerable about potential threat and overreact like Chicken Little to a non-existent danger. You may be scattering your energies and jumping to conclusions when the threat may well blow over if you wait it out. With the **Moon, 5 of Swords,** or **7 of Swords,** you may underestimate your ability to cope with the miscommunications or manipulations of others.

THE NINE OF PENTACLES
(Comfortable Home)

UPRIGHT MEANING: A woman who ressembles Rita Hayworth sits at the window of her elegant estate holding its key in her hand. Birds, beautiful flowers, and the grounds of her gardens are visible beyond her window while fruit, wine, and nine pentacles grace the interior of her home. These images convey the enjoyment of animals, plants, and a beautiful home environment. This card is very favorable for all kinds of real estate dealings - commercial, residential, raw land, or business locations. With the **Empress**, the setting may be lush and beautiful and the interior lavish, such as an elegant hotel or house in the country. Traditionally, this card related to comfort and affluence, usually enjoyed by someone who enjoyed privacy or living alone.

Example Situation: A painter leases an historic farmhouse in the country.

IN A SPREAD: You have a home and lifestyle that bring joy and comfort to you. With the **Empress**, you may want to enhance your environment by landscaping, redecorating, or adding a pool or hot tub. Your home may feel like a safe haven and retreat from the world but you may spend too much time alone there, if the **Hermit R** also appears in the spread.

Example Situation: A woman finds that maintaining a 100 year old home is too expensive and puts it in the market.

REVERSED MEANING: You may have some financial losses or upsets relating to your home or office or be forced to find a new location. The **7 of Swords** or the **Moon** can indicate burglary or slipshod house repairs. With the **10 of Pentacles**, **Sun**, or **6 of Pentacles**, you may successfully sell your house or find a new location.

Tens

The Ten of any suit represents renewal through a new cycle and mastery of lessons regarding the suit in question. With Swords, the cycle ends in disaster. With Cups, love is the outcome. The Ten of Wands represents stress and pressure, while the Ten of Pentacles stands for material prosperity.

THE TEN OF SWORDS
(Disaster)

UPRIGHT MEANING: This card depicts a man shrieking in terror as ten swords fly through the air around him. These are effective symbols for an utterly devastating situation — one without further recourse. Unlike the impending doom of the 9 of Swords, the 10 of Swords is the final acceptance of a hopeless impasse. There is no choice but to abandon the futile direction and regroup from disaster. Often, this feels like a relief because the effort to continue with the struggle is released. By surrendering to the inevitable failure of the situation, new forms can arise from the rubble. With the **3 of Swords** or the **4 of Wands R**, a divorce may be inevitable. Financial devastation or bankruptcy are indicated with the **10 of Pentacles R** or the **Tower**.

Example Situation: A penniless teenager who has been living on the streets realizes that she will die if she doesn't seek help.

IN A SPREAD: You are well aware of the futility of continuing with a disastrous direction in your life. You know you must abandon it and choose another path with room for hope and new growth. Take the steps to close the door on the destructive path remembering to focus energy on the new paths that offer inspiration to you. Resolve to leave your distress behind by acting now and learn the lessons that are the gift of this difficult period.

Example Situation: A woman rebuilds her life after declaring bankruptcy.

REVERSED MEANING: Congratulate yourself on surviving a devastating loss and marshall your courage and determination to forge ahead. You have learned from your ordeal and will not repeat the mistakes that led to disaster. The loss you have survived is something you feared and felt you could not endure. You have proven that you could cope with even your worst fears. You can move ahead knowing that you are stronger for the ordeal.

THE TEN OF CUPS
(Love)

UPRIGHT MEANING: A contented woman sits contemplating ten overflowing cups that surround her. A waterfall cascades in the distance. The water symbols describe the full expression of emotional happiness and love through deep intimacy and rapport. The relationship may be a romantic or sexual one with the **Lovers** or **7 of Cups** also in the spread. It may symbolize a family or group with total unconditional love among its members with the **3 of Cups** or **6 of Cups**. With the **Lovers**, it shows the depth and intensity of emotional sharing that soulmates feel for each other. The deepest love for a child is indicated with the **Princess of Cups** or the **Empress** in the spread.

Example Situation: After therapy to heal abandonment by her parents, a woman is able to share her deepest feelings with her husband.

IN A SPREAD: Those you love care deeply about you and want to be there for you. You are blessed with family, friends, or groups who have healed emotional wounds and are open and caring. You are able to receive the loving warmth of those close to you and are generous and caring in your interactions with others.

Example Situation: A couple get caught up in their jobs and neglects the tender expressions of their love.

REVERSED MEANING: This card can indicate a close connection that has lost some of its depth and openness because of neglect or distance. It can also pertain to one-sided relationships in which one of the parties feels a deeper connection than the other. In a previously "perfect" relationship, disagreements or incompatible interests can be blemishing the level of rapport.

THE TEN OF WANDS
(Stress and Pressure)

UPRIGHT MEANING: A man surrounded by ten wands crumbles to the ground as flames engulf the scene around him. The planet Saturn signifying limitation and pressure is visible overhead. The desperation pictured in this card is often the result of excessive responsibilities and pressures. Workaholism may be burdening life with drudgery. There is a strong need to decrease the stress through exercise, hobbies, or recreation. Hiring an assistant or taking a vacation may help bring a greater balance between work and play. There is a hidden perfectionism implied in this card because of the unbridled drive to tackle too many responsibilities singlehandedly.

Example Situation: A harried mother of five children rarely takes any time off for herself.

IN A SPREAD: You feel burdened with crushing responsibilities at times and need to look for ways to lighten up your load. You may be showing your level of stress through irritability or resentment if the **5 of Swords** or **7 of Swords** also appear in the spread. With the **Emperor R** or **Magician R**, your authority may have gone to your head and you may be treating others in a high-handed manner. You need a break so that you can realize the proper place of duty in your life.

Example Situation: After a marathon schedule of overtime, a man realizes that the extra money was not worth the toll it took on his life in terms of pressure.

REVERSED MEANING: You are experiencing relief because the burdens and pressures of your life have eased and there is more time for fun and relaxation. You may have learned from previous overwork and worry that you can take care of your needs without a life of drudgery. With the **Hanged Man R**, you are no longer taking on others' problems as your own

THE TEN OF PENTACLES
(Material Prosperity)

UPRIGHT MEANING: A richly dressed man in an elegant mansion stands surrounded by ten pentacles holding a dove. This picture conveys both the financial security of the lavish setting and the serenity of the dove. This card can relate to money acquired through family inheritance or corporate wealth and is a positive indicator for attracting financial prosperity through inheritance, investments, or big business deals. The amount of money represented by this card will vary for a rich or poor person but will feel like a large sum of money to each. With the **9 of Pentacles**, it can be favorable for making large purchases, such as acreage or developed real estate. With positive cards, emotional satisfaction accompanies the material prosperity described by this card. With the **Devil**, there is danger of greed and immersion in material values.

Example Situation: A woman buys a beautiful home with her inheritance.

IN A SPREAD: You are well-protected financially and can expect your prosperity to continue. With the **Empress**, **Sun**, **Ace of Pentacles**, or the **Magician**, you may want to expand your holdings in a new direction, possibly an innovative one.

Example Situation: A businessman loses heavily when the stock market takes a sharp decline.

REVERSED: Here, there can be serious problems regarding an inheritance or business dealings. Financial reversals or investment losses are likely with the **Tower** or **Wheel of Fortune R**. You may need to liquidate some of your assets or otherwise restructure your finances to resolve the losses. With **Justice R** or **Judgement R**, an inheritance dispute may go against you in the courts.

The Court Cards

Overview

The Court Cards correspond to the face cards in an ordinary deck. They usually represent people in our lives rather than situations or events.

- The **Princesses** can represent either messages or young people up to the age of 25 of either sex.
- The **Princes** represent action or men between the ages of 25 and 40.
- The **Queens** signify women over the age of 25.
- The **Kings** deal with men over the age of 40.

When a Court Card appears in a spread, you can try to determine who that card stands for by associating its suit with physical appearance or astrological sign. The suits tell us the hair and eye coloring of the Court Cards.

- The coloring for **Swords** is medium brown hair and light eyes. For example, the Princess of Swords is a medium-haired, light-eyed young person under age 25. The Prince of Swords is a medium-haired, light-eyed man between ages 25 and 40. The Queen of Swords is a woman over age 25 with medium hair and light eyes. The King of Swords is a medium-haired man with light eyes over age 40.
- The coloring for **Cups** is blond or gray hair and light eyes.
- The coloring for **Wands** is sandy or reddish hair, light or freckled skin, and dark or light eyes.
- The coloring for **Pentacles** is dark hair, skin, and eyes. This suit can represent blacks or other dark-skinned ethnic groups.

The four suits of the Minor Arcana can also be related to the earth, air, fire, and water signs in astrology.

- The **Swords** correspond to the air signs which are Gemini, Libra, and Aquarius. When reading a Sword Court Card, you might want to describe the person astrologically as an air sign rather than use hair and eye coloring.
- The **Cups** correspond to the water signs in astrology which are Cancer, Scorpio, and Pisces.

- The **Wands** correspond to the fire signs which are Aries, Leo, and Sagittarius.
- The **Pentacles** correspond to the earth signs which are Taurus, Virgo, and Capricorn.

This means that when you are describing a person who is represented in the cards, for example, by the Knight of Swords, you would say that he is brown-haired and light-eyed *or* that his astrological sign may be Gemini, Libra, or Aquarius. In some cases, the physical appearance and astrological sign will both fit the same Court Card when describing the person. Decide before you shuffle whether you are using coloring or astrological signs to describe people who appear in the spread.

Ages of Court Cards

Princess - young person of either sex, aged 0-25

Prince - man aged 25-40

Queen - woman over 25

King - man over 40

Coloring of Suits

Swords - brown hair and light eyes

Cups - blond or gray hair and light eyes

Wands - sandy or reddish hair

Pentacles - dark hair, eyes, and skin (blacks or foreigners)

Astrological Signs of Suits

Swords - air signs (Gemini, Libra, Aquarius)

Cups - water signs (Cancer, Scorpio, Pisces)

Wands - fire signs (Aries, Leo, Sagittarius)

Pentacles - earth signs (Taurus, Virgo, Capricorn)

Princesses

The Princess of any suit represents either a message or a young person under the age of 25. With the Sword suit, the message is one of forceful communication. With Cups, the message is social. The Princess of Wands represents an enthusiastic message, while the Princess of Pentacles is a message about financial dealings.

THE PRINCESS OF SWORDS
(Forceful Communication)

UPRIGHT MEANING: A young woman holding a sword stares intently ahead. She wears crystal and diamond jewelry symbolizing the sharp clarity of her communications. An eagle symbolizing Scorpio appears in the foreground. When it describes a young person under the age of 25, he or she may be a Gemini, Libra, or Aquarian by astrological sign or brown-haired and light eyed by coloring. The temperament of the person would be logical and mental. This card relates to direct, no-nonsense interactions between people. The message may appear blunt but there is no mistaking the intent. The tone of the communication is mental, precise, and intense, similar to a lawyer's approach to presenting his arguments. It can refer to a legal summons with **Justice** or **Judgement** or to constructive criticism with the **3 of Pentacles**.

Example Situation: A young woman enjoys discussing her interest in social justice with others on a computer network.

IN A SPREAD: You may need to defuse an awkward situation by bringing it out in the open with straight talk about it. Often, facing a challenging exchange with another person is a relief and clears the air. A young person with the qualities of the Princess of Swords may enter your life to help you express your own ability to speak your truth.

Example Situation: An employer is harsh and disrespectful in his interactions with his employees.

REVERSED MEANING: Your communications with others are forceful and matter-of-fact and may lack the human element. This is an instance where *what* you say could be resented if you are not conscious of *how* you are saying it. Communications with a young person may be at cross purposes until hostility and resistance have been addressed.

THE PRINCESS OF CUPS
(Social Messages)

UPRIGHT MEANING: A dreamy young Greta Garbo wearing moonstone jewelry rests her hands on a golden cup. She wears a wedding band symbolizing her emotional loyalty to others. An iris and a sailing vessel further relate to her gentle romantic nature as a water sign. When this card refers to a young person under 25, he or she may be a Cancer, Scorpio, or Pisces by astrological sign or have light hair and eyes by coloring. The temperament is emotionally sensitive, gentle, and kind. The Princess of Cups represents both children and gay people. This card also relates to social invitations, friendly phone calls, and personal letters.

Example Situation: A sensitive child tells his mother about a happy dream he had about his upcoming birthday party.

IN A SPREAD: A sensitive child or gay person can bring you joy now and help you reconnect to your own ability to trust and open up emotionally. When this card does not relate to a person in your life, it indicates benefit from contacting loved ones by phone, letter, or through social gatherings.

Example Situation: A woman suspends her social interactions while she finishes writing her book.

REVERSED MEANING: You may not hear from your friends or family at this time and experience a slowdown of social invitations. You may prefer to back off from others and spend time pursuing interests on your own. With the **Hermit R**, you may be avoiding social contacts and spending too much time alone.

THE PRINCESS OF WANDS
(Enthusiasm)

UPRIGHT MEANING: A lively young woman wearing the symbol of fire on her golden tiara and holding a wand expresses the vitality of the sun in the distance. As a person, this card symbolizes a creative and exuberant young person under the age of 25, who is fiery by temperament (Aries, Leo, or Sagittarius) or sandy or reddish haired, light or dark eyed, with light freckled skin. Because of his or her high energy, the Princess of Wands thrives on adventurous, athletic, and enterprising activities. This card can also signify good news that creates a feeling of enthusiasm and inspiration.

Example Situation: An enterprising young man receives the news that his new software idea has been accepted by a major software company.

IN A SPREAD: You may receive exciting good news or hear about an idea that fascinates you and could become a new interest in your life. You can inspire others and foster their creativity at this time. A young person with a bubbly personality may bring greater humor and adventure into your life.

Example Situation: A young man hastily assembles a new bicycle without reading the directions and has to start over.

REVERSED MEANING: The young person may be cocky and impatient, with a quick temper. He or she may tend to be flighty, disorganized, and hard-headed. You may feel angry and impatient about delays or irritable and volatile in your communications. You may hear some news that is unpleasant and upsetting.

PRINCESS OF PENTACLES
(Financial Dealings)

UPRIGHT MEANING: A dark young woman is surrounded by an earthy setting of mountains, ferns, and a mountain goat (Capricorn). She wears a Taurus symbol on her headband and a pentacle on her breast symbolizing her connection to practicality and concrete reality. As a person, the Princess of Pentacles is a conscientious, goal-oriented young person under the age of 25. He or she may be an earth sign (Taurus, Virgo, or Capricorn) or have dark coloring, with dark eyes, hair, and complexion. This card also relates to all communications pertaining to money and business dealings, such as proposals, transactions, and contracts. Business meetings, phone calls, memos, and discussions express the flow of business and commerce that the Princess of Pentacles signifies. With positive cards, this card pertains to good messages about money or business.

Example Situation: A serious-minded young sculpture student learns of her acceptance in a summer apprenticeship program at a foundry.

IN A SPREAD: You may receive good news about financial matters or business proposals. A favorable contract is likely with **Justice** or **Judgement** in the same spread. With the **Hermit**, you may act as a mentor for a scholarly young person. Renewing contacts with business connections can produce favorable results.

Example Situation: A young sales representative worries about paying her bills after a month of low sales.

REVERSED MEANING: A slowdown in business activities and sales could create a financial crunch for you. You may hear some disappointing news about your business prospects. If you have mismanaged your money, now is the time to put your financial affairs in order. A young person may be worried about money or feel insecure about handling school or work duties.

Princes

The Prince of any suit represents a man between the ages of 25 and 40. With the Sword suit, the person is assertive, and possibly an air sign with medium hair and light eyes. With Cups, the person is congenial, and may be a water sign with blond or gray hair and light eyes. The Prince of Wands is an energetic, fire sign person with sandy or reddish hair, while the Prince of Pentacles is a shrewd, earth sign person with dark hair, eyes, and skin.

THE PRINCE OF SWORDS
(Assertive Action)

UPRIGHT MEANING: A man wearing the symbol of Aquarius holds a sword in one hand and a book in the other. A falcon peers around his right shoulder. The symbols on this card describe a mentally astute person who respects knowledge and can use his sharp intellect assertively. When this card represents a person, he is a man between the ages of 25-40 with medium hair and light eyes or who is an air sign (Gemini, Libra, or Aquarius). This Prince relates to action of a mental nature, implying a show of conviction reinforced by firm and decisive action.

Example Situation: A well-informed and articulate man challenges a zoning change at a city council meeting.

IN A SPREAD: The Prince of Swords is often a person who is direct and confrontive and who encourages you to act upon your ideas. When this card does not relate to a person in your life, it can show a part of yourself that enjoys challenging intellectual discussions. Bouncing ideas off another person now can fortify your convictions and prepare you to defend them if necessary.

Example Situation: An angry and abrasive man alienates others with his "know-it-all" attitude.

REVERSED MEANING: This card represents a sarcastic person who disrespectfully forces his opinions on others. He may interrupt constantly or be a poor listener. He could be fanatically caught up in radical ideas that promote violence and fear. When it does not represent a hostile and reckless person to avoid, this card can show that your judgment has been impaired by reactionary thinking. Put things in perspective and get centered emotionally before taking action.

THE PRINCE OF CUPS
(Congeniality)

UPRIGHT MEANING: The Prince of Cups appears as Alain Delon in this card with his intense Scorpionic gaze reflected in the scorpion and a glowing snake rising from a cup. Through emotional transformation, he has shed his old skin like the snake and received insight. This card represents a man between the ages of 25 and 40, with light hair and eyes or who is a water sign (Cancer, Scorpio, or Pisces). He is charming and likeable, with an empathetic and warm personality. He is open emotionally and relates especially well to women for this reason. He is drawn to "people" jobs such as counseling, sales, public relations, or customer service. When it does not relate to a person, this card can refer to social invitations.

Example Situation: A popular young man organizes the office Christmas party.

IN A SPREAD: A personable man could benefit you personally or professionally through his social finesse and emotional sincerity. He can be a loyal and sympathetic friend and has an instinct for soothing others' feelings. In a woman's spread, a man may let her know that he is attracted to her or ask her for a date.

Example Situation: A man at a singles' bar turns on the charm in order to seduce a woman.

REVERSED MEANING: Here, the person is manipulative and insincere, saying what the other person wants to hear to get his way. He may pride himself on his conquests as a "Ladies Man" but find it impossible to have a deep and lasting relationship with friends or lovers. Even though he may have a slick veneer, people soon realize that he is superficial and self-serving.

THE PRINCE OF WANDS
(Energy)

UPRIGHT MEANING: The Prince of Wands has the features of Tom Cruise and wears an emblem of the sign Leo, carrying a regal shield decorated with the face of a lion. The brilliant sun above reflects from the fire emblem on his headband. The person described by this card is a man 25-40 years old, with sandy or reddish hair and freckled skin or a fire sign (Aries, Leo, or Sagittarius). He is lively, athletic, spontaneous, and loves being on the move. He enjoys adventure and excitement and can engage in dangerous enterprises. This card signifies dynamic movement and energy. It is one of the traditional cards for travel or a change of residence when combined with the **Fool, 6 of Swords, World, 8 of Wands**, or the **Wheel of Fortune**.

Example Situation: A man spontaneously hops on a plane for Las Vegas for the weekend.

IN A SPREAD: If you do not have the card combinations for travel or a change of residence, an energetic and confident man may bring new enthusiasm and adventure into your life. This card could also describe a need for more spontaneous action, physical exercise, or travel in your life.

Example Situation: A man hotly pursues a woman he barely knows even though she has given him no encouragement.

REVERSED MEANING: You may delay a trip or a change of residence if other combination cards for travel appear in the spread. You could become irritable and scattered because of time constraints. An impatient, pushy man may try to railroad you into hasty action or push his affections on you. With the **7 of Swords** or **3 of Swords**, he may be a jealous and suspicious person.

THE PRINCE OF PENTACLES
(Shrewd Business Activities)

UPRIGHT MEANING: The Prince of Pentacles with the features of Charles Bronson wears a pentacle on his shirt and resonates to a goat in the background through the sign Capricorn. He represents a dark-haired, dark-eyed man between 25 and 40 with an earth sign temperament (Taurus, Virgo, Capricorn). He is hardworking, conscientious, and astute in business matters. He bases his decisions on common sense and practicality rather than wishful thinking. He is not a gambler at heart and chooses low risk investments. He is more of a saver than a spender although he values quality when he buys. He could be a loyal and reliable friend or business associate who offers excellent financial advice. He prefers to accept life as it is rather than to question its meaning. When this card does not refer to a person, it relates to decisive actions involving money and business.

Example Situation: A businessman is constantly alert for money-making opportunities that offer solid financial growth to him.

IN A SPREAD: A down-to-earth but predictable man may enter your life to show you how to take sound financial action in your life. He may also expose you to nature through his interest in the earth and natural sciences. If this card does not refer to a person, it indicates that it's time to get off hold and move on financial matters.

Example Situation: An obsessed but unproductive worker worries constantly about money and has no social life.

REVERSED MEANING: Here, the Prince has become a pauper through his insecurity and poverty consciousness. He is inefficient in his work, overdoing minor tasks while never getting around to the most important projects. He is critical of others at work but blind to his own incompetency. When this card does not refer to a person, it represents delays and hassles regarding business and money matters.

Queens

The Queen of any suit represents a woman over the age of 25. With the Sword suit, the person is strong-willed, and possibly an air sign with medium hair and light eyes. With Cups, the person is nurturing, and may be a water sign with blond or gray hair and light eyes. The Queen of Wands is an exuberant, fire sign person with sandy or reddish hair, while the Queen of Pentacles is a practical, earth sign person with dark hair, eyes, and skin.

THE QUEEN OF SWORDS
(Strong-Willed)

UPRIGHT MEANING: A woman wearing diamonds and crystals holds a sword and wears the astrological symbols for Gemini on her cape and the symbol for Mercury on her throne. From her window, two lovers embrace in a country setting. A white bird representing serenity keeps her company. The Queen of Swords closely ressembles Ingrid Bergman and carries the cool confidence of her image. Her glance is almost challenging others to show her respect for her intelligence, wit, and education or suffer the consequences of her sharp tongue. Traditionally, the Queen of Swords was a widow or divorced woman, who had developed strength from suffering disappointment in love and enduring hardship. The lovers pictured in the background may show her past passions and her self-protection from being hurt again. The Queen of Swords represents a woman over 25 who may have medium hair and light eyes or be an air sign (Gemini, Libra, or Aquarius).

Example Situation: A woman lawyer is a formidable opponent in court.

IN A SPREAD: You may have a friend who displays the feisty, self-reliant qualities of the Queen of Swords. She can be a powerful ally, using her mental prowess and wit in defense of her loved ones. She can also be intimidating to men because she projects a tough exterior that hides her fragile emotional side. It often takes time for acquaintances and potential lovers to look past her defensiveness to enjoy her lively mind and humor.

Example Situation: A woman executive humiliates a male employee with sarcasm and criticism in a department meeting.

REVERSED MEANING: This card relates to a bad-tempered woman who has become embittered and vengeful. She is driven by her envy and jealousy of others whom she sees as threats to her ego. She competes with other women rather than seeing them as potential friends. With men, she may be passive-aggressive, using subtle manipulation to try to dominate.

THE QUEEN OF CUPS
(Nurturing)

UPRIGHT MEANING: A woman wearing a tiara with the trident of Neptune and the yin/yang symbol holds a fan decorated with the two fish representing Pisces. Her beauty suggests the sensitivity of Greta Garbo. She wears a Star of David pendant symbolizing her ability to balance the material and spiritual realms. A cup of gentleness and kindness glows beside her and a peaceful pond glistens in the background. The Queen of Cups traditionally relates to the personal mother as opposed to the Empress who is the collective Earth Mother. She is a woman over the age of 25 with light or gray hair and light eyes or who is a water sign (Cancer, Scorpio, or Pisces). She is emotionally sensitive and empathetic, enjoying nurturing others through listening and counseling. She is idealistic about love and yearns to find her fulfillment through "true love." She thrives in her roles as mother, wife, or devoted friend.

Example Situation: A kind woman takes a basket of fruit to a sick neighbor.

IN A SPREAD: Draw upon the loving energy of a sweet and caring woman around you. She may be your mother or a friend who is accepting and open-hearted. You will find a welcome confidant in the Queen of Cups for emotional issues you may need to discuss.

Example Situation: A well-meaning but co-dependent mother allows her grown son to lead an irresponsible life by providing for all his needs.

REVERSED MEANING: Here, the Queen of Cups is disconnected from her ability to nurture with wisdom and intuition. She allows herself to be used for emotional support by those attached to being victims without taking responsibility for their own lives. She may confuse sentimentality with caring and choose self-absorbed people as intimates. She may project a sweet but naive image to others and lack semotional maturity and depth.

THE QUEEN OF WANDS
(Exuberance)

UPRIGHT MEANING: A tempestuous woman ressembling Elizabeth Taylor holds the wand of creativity while the Sagittarian archer standing on a tower in the background draws his bow. The Queen of Wands is a woman over 25 years of age who is sandy or reddish-haired or a fire sign (Aries, Leo, or Sagittarius). She is lively, impulsive, and driven by enthusiasm to explore life adventurously. She can be an ardent lover, but also hot-headed and emotionally volatile. She is independent and creative, with an enterprising spirit in business. She is extraverted and bubbly in social situations and the fire of her personality lights up a room when she enters.

Example Situation: An opera singer performs an encore after enchanting her audience.

IN A SPREAD: You can add sparkle to your life through a woman with a bubbly personality now. She may inspire you with her confidence and zest for life to take the steps to express your creativity. She may stimulate a desire to take a trip or to enjoy nature through hikes or sports.

Example Situation: A harried graphic artist throws a temper tantrum when she cannot find a drawing in the heaps of papers on her desk.

REVERSED MEANING: This card refers to a talented but scattered woman, who overextends herself constantly and then panics at the pressure she is under. Because she is not grounded and organized, she is often harried, irritable, and late for appointments. She can become frantic about small annoyances even to the point of hysteria. Her anger and tears arise spontaneously under stress. She tends to talks fast and may do most of the talking in a conversation without listening well.

THE QUEEN OF PENTACLES
(Practicality)

UPRIGHT MEANING: A woman near a castle in the forest holds a rose from which a pentacle emerges. The Queen of Pentacles is a woman over 25 years old, who has dark hair, eyes, and skin or who is an earth sign (Taurus, Virgo, or Capricorn). She is practical and astute in business. She focuses on her financial ambitions and career goals. Her resourcefulness and gift for organization help her to climb the ladder of success rapidly. While she is a go-getter in business, she is also very sensual and earthy in love.

Example Situation: An ambitious real estate saleswoman sells a million dollars in property her first year.

IN A SPREAD: A woman of this description could give you excellent business advice or represent you in a financial situation. She is knowledgeable and well-grounded in her field and can explain her area of expertise in a down-to-earth way.

Example Situation: A woman attends a class on "How to Marry a Rich Husband."

REVERSED MEANING: This woman is the snob who values social status, money, and power above all else. She is more than likely both a social climber and a name dropper seeking to hide her insecurities by inspiring envy in others. The people in her life are an extension of her ego s and must have the "right" education, address, car, job, and labels.

Kings

The King of any suit represents a man over the age of 40. With the Sword suit, the person is intelligent, and possibly an air sign with medium hair and light eyes. With Cups, the person is protective, and may be a water sign with blond or gray hair and light eyes. The King of Wands is an entrepreneurial, fire sign person with sandy or reddish hair, while the King of Pentacles possesses business ability and is an earth sign person with dark hair, eyes, and skin.

THE KING OF SWORDS
(Intelligence)

UPRIGHT MEANING: A crowned man wears the emblem for Libra on his chest and carries a sword. A white falcon symbolizing mental clarity accompanies him. The King of Swords is a man over 40 who has dark hair and light eyes or who is an air sign (Gemini, Libra, or Aquarius). He is a man of strong intellect with a keen and curious mind. He is a man whose leadership abilities stem from his mental clarity and conviction. He enjoys the lively exchange of ideas and will defend his point of view adamantly. His wide range of interests makes him a good conversationalist. He values education and has likely acquired advanced degrees. He is admired and respected in his field for his objectivity and quick grasp of new concepts. Because he is able to see ideas from a logical, legalistic point of view, he would make a good lawyer or judge.

Example Situation: A Supreme Court judge writes his decision after careful consideration.

IN A SPREAD: You may encounter a man who enjoys mental challenges or solving puzzles and keeps you on your toes. A man with a brilliant intellect can give you valuable advice about matters of concern to you. He may be a professional man such as a doctor or lawyer, especially if the spread involves medical or legal matters.

Example Situation: An arrogant, loud-mouthed union leader threatens to call a strike without attempting negotiations.

REVERSED MEANING: The King of Swords has become verbally abusive and demeaning in his communications, alienating others. He intentionally challenges others' ideas so that he can shout them down with his dogmatic opinions. He uses his intelligence to manipulate others like pawns in a chess game without regard for their personal feelings. Because the **King of Swords R** is cut off from his heart, he misuses his intellectual gifts and drives away the love he needs from others.

THE KING OF CUPS
(Protective)

UPRIGHT MEANING: A crowned man surrounded by symbols for the astrological sign Cancer (crab, crescent moon, and glyph) enjoys an exotic seaside palace. He closely ressembles Clark Gable and holds an ornate shimmering cup. The King of Cups is a kindly man over 40 who has light or gray hair and eyes or who is a water sign (Cancer, Scorpio, or Pisces). He is emotionally sensitive and protective of those close to him. He enjoys expressing his feelings and listening to others' troubles sympathetically. He has a lively imagination and vivid dream life. He may be drawn to work in the helping professions as a minister or counselor. The Emperor relates to the archetype of the father while the King of Cups pertains to the personal father.

Example Situation: An older man acts as a mentor for a young man without a father.

IN A SPREAD: Your own father or a father figure may relate to your question. Psychological issues could be involved, especially with the Emperor upright or reversed in the same spread. Consulting a sensitive older man for comfort and advice could help you clear some emotional turbulence.

Example Situation: An older man tells stories from his youth and gives unsolicited advice to young people at a local bar.

REVERSED MEANING: Here, the King of Cups has become sentimental and maudlin without the balance of mental objectivity. He may foster the weakness of others by enabling them to continue destructive behavior. He has not learned to combine empathy with wisdom in his desire to help others. He may be a heavy drinker who goes to emotional extremes when he is "in his cups."

THE KING OF WANDS
(Entrepreneur)

UPRIGHT MEANING: A man ressembling Sean Connery wears a crown and holds a golden wand. His staff bearing the symbol for Aries stands in the background and a red tulip appears in the foreground. The King of Wands is a confident man over 40 with sandy or reddish hair and light or dark eyes. He may be a fire sign (Aries, Leo, or Sagittarius) with creative vision and an enterprising nature. He enjoys taking risks by embarking on entrepreneurial ventures. His gifts for motivating and inspiring others make him well-suited for a career in sales, marketing, promotions, or advertising. He loves travel and adventure and prefers spontaneity in his work to a scheduled routine.

Example Situation: An advertising copywriter designs a magazine ad for a new product.

IN A SPREAD: You may feel inspired and encouraged from contact with a dynamic and optimistic man around you. He may help you to believe in the potential for your own ideas and give you ideas for promoting yourself. He may have an idea or product that captures your imagination. His vision and enthusiasm are infectious and offer new inspiration in your life.

Example Situation: A compulsive gambler is obsessed with getting rich quick.

REVERSED MEANING: Here, the King is an impatient, temperamental person who charges into risky ventures without good sense. He is always hoping for the lucky break that will redeem all the money he has lost through his foolishness. He lacks the patience to carry any of his good ideas forward to the point of success. He may use his gifts for persuasion to con others out of their money with promises of quick money.

THE KING OF PENTACLES
(Business Ability)

UPRIGHT MEANING: A richly dressed man wearing a crown ressembles Gregory Peck and smiles as he counts his pentacles in his elegant palace. The goat symbol for Capricorn appears on a ridge in the background. The King of Pentacles is a dark-haired, dark-eyed man or an earth sign (Taurus, Virgo, or Capricorn). He is practical and business-oriented by nature and likely to be successful. He gravitates toward careers in financial areas, such as banking, stocks and bonds, accounting, or real estate. He enjoys the everyday commerce of the marketplace and may own his own business. He loves to plan for the practical needs of the future and is loyal, dependable, and trustworthy.

Example Situation: A businessman starts out with a single retail outlet and builds it into a franchise operation.

IN A SPREAD: Business advice from the King of Pentacles could help you make solid business decisions and plan for the future. His common sense and business expertise are well-grounded in experience and can help you build security.

Example Situation: A disorganized and absent-minded manager struggles to cope with the crises his mismanagement has created.

REVERSED MEANING: This card refers to a man who desperately wants material prosperity but whose success is elusive because he neglects the details of his business. His lack of good business sense results in poor decisions in such areas as hiring, inventory, and advertising. He may prefer to fly by the seat of his pants in business, wheeling and dealing without substance or carry through.

Combinations

Major events and life changes appear in a Tarot spread as a combination of cards rather than just one or two cards. For events of the magnitude of marriage, birth, illness, or death, the likelihood increases with each additional card reinforcing the event.

The following list shows certain combinations that indicate specific meanings. You should see at least two or three of the cards shown in the combination before interpreting them as listed. For example, the combination for ill health is the 4 of Swords, 8 of Swords, Sun R, and Star R. You would not predict ill health unless two, but more likely, three or more of the above cards were together in the spread.

Since the Tarot reflects the *probable* future direction of events, special care must be taken to empower others rather than frighten them about upcoming events. By tactfully expressing a possible worsening of conditions if nothing intervenes, even bad news can be communicated in a helpful manner. If you saw the combination for ill health in a spread, it would be best to ask the person if he has any health problems and warn him to pay special attention to health in the near future.

ABUSIVE FAMILY CONDITIONS	Three of Swords Four of Wands R Ten of Pentacles R Tower Death
ADDICTION	Three of Cups R Seven of Cups Temperance R Moon Hanged Man
ANDROGENY, HOMOSEXUALITY	Princess of Cups Queens (for males) Kings or Princes (for females)

ANGER	Three of Swords Five of Swords Five of Wands Ace of Swords R Ten of Cups R
BETRAYAL	Five of Swords Seven of Swords Three of Swords Moon
BLACK MAGIC, SELFISHNESS	Devil Wheel of Fortune R Magician R Judgement R
CHANGE OF RESIDENCE	Four of Wands R Nine of Pentacles R Prince of Wands Tower
COMMUNITY	Three of Cups Six of Cups Nine of Pentacles Star Three of Wands
ENLIGHTENMENT	Ace of Pentacles Ace of Cups Star Tower Magician High Priestess
FINANCIAL INSECURITY	Five of Pentacles Seven of Pentacles R Tower Wheel of Fortune R
GENEROSITY, BENEVOLENCE	Six of Pentacles Seven of Pentacles Sun Empress

HEALER, RETURN TO HEALTH	Four of Swords R Star Sun Strength Hierophant
ILL HEALTH	Four of Swords Eight of Swords Sun R Star R
INNOVATION	Chariot Magician Hierophant R Star Ace of Wands
JOB, QUITTING	5 of Pentacles Three of Swords High Swords (Eight, Nine, or Ten) Eight of Cups
KARMIC GIFTS	Six of Cups Six of Pentacles Empress
LAW AND JUSTICE	Five of Wands Judgement Justice Emperor
LEADERSHIP	Emperor Chariot Star Sun
MANIFESTATION	Six of Wands Nine of Cups Star Sun Ten of Pentacles

MARRIAGE	Three of Cups Four of Wands Ten of Pentacles Ten of Cups Lovers
MEDITATION	Hermit High Priestess Star Magician
MODERATION	Seven of Cups R Strength Devil R Temperance Justice
MONEY, GOOD LUCK	Pentacles Six of Pentacles Sun Wheel of Fortune
MONEY, KARMIC LESSONS	Seven of Swords Seven of Pentacles R Nine of Pentacles R Ten of Pentacles R Sun R Empress R
MONEY, WEALTH	Nine of Pentacles Ten of Pentacles Sun Empress Emperor
MOTHER	Three of Cups Six of Cups Princess of Cups Empress Queen of Cups

NEAR DEATH EXPERIENCE	Four of Swords Ten of Swords Death Tower Star
RESEARCH, STUDY	Three of Pentacles Eight of Pentacles Hermit Princess of Pentacles
SUCCESSFUL NEW VENTURE	Ace of Pentacles Chariot Empress Ten of Pentacles
SUICIDAL DEPRESSION	Three of Swords Eight of Swords Nine of Swords Tower Star R
THEFT	Pentacles Five of Swords Seven of Swords Nine of Pentacles R Moon
TRAVEL	Six of Swords Eight of Wands Prince of Wands World Fool Wheel of Fortune Chariot
VIOLENCE, TRAUMA	Eight of Swords Nine of Swords Ten of Swords Chariot R Five of Wands Three of Swords Ace of Swords R

WOMEN'S SPIRITUALITY   Empress
                                  High Priestess
                                  Three of Cups
                                  Six of Cups
                                  Strength
                                  Three of Wands

Reading Spreads

The Purpose of Spreads

The positions of the cards when they are laid out provide specific information based upon their position in the layout or "spread." Often, there is a position for the past, present, and future of the question being asked. The most helpful spreads are those that deepen insight by providing access to hidden areas for self-awareness. Since my approach to Tarot card reading seeks to empower the person asking the question, I do not emphasize the predictive aspects of the Tarot. My philosophy is to trigger new areas of insight so that the questioner can stay focused on the meaning and purpose of everyday existence.

The Timing and Advice Cards

In the past, confusion arose about the scope of a spread's message because it was difficult to determine the timing that applied to a spread. A card to sum up the best action or attitude for the present time was also missing from most Tarot spreads. I have created a timing system and added both timing and advice cards to my spreads to help determine when a situation will change and what the best approach might be for the present time.

Timing

The timing card gives the time interval covered by the spread. The suit indicates whether the duration is a matter of days, weeks, or months:

Cups — days
Wands — weeks
Pentacles — months

The number of the card indicates the number of days, weeks, or months involved:

Ace through Ten — one through ten
Princess — eleven
Prince — twelve

To determine the timing, combine the suit and numerical value of the card. For example, the Princess of Cups in the timing position is 11 days, the 7 of Wands is 7 weeks.

Page 127

If any of the following appears in the timing position, timing cannot be pinpointed at this time or is up to the discretion of the questioner:

Swords — undetermined, up to you

Queen — undetermined, up to you

King — undetermined, up to you

If a Major Arcana card falls in the timing position, it indicates that the questioner is involved in an ongoing psychological or spiritual process. The process has already begun, is proceeding in the present, and is likely to continue for at least six more weeks.

Major Arcana — now

If the timing card is very immediate, such as the next two weeks, notice the advice of the cards position for immediate suggestions. Usually, very immediate timing shows quick resolution to a problem or the need to focus on a personal growth issue in the near future that will impact timing over the long haul. The Major Arcana cards in the spread will often describe the lesson involved.

It is not necessary to interpret the meaning of the timing card, but often the card that falls there is very appropriate to the situation.

The Advice of the Cards

The "advice of the cards" position tells you the best approach or attitude to take about the question asked. Since many spreads provide so much information, it helps to have one card that simplifies and summarizes the best approach to take right now about the issue.

The Star of Insight Spread

The Star of Insight Spread is an all purpose spread and can be used to provide detailed information and insight into almost any question. The diagram for this spread shows both the meanings of the positions and the order in which you lay the cards out, beginning with 1 and ending with 11.

Meanings of Positions in the Spread

As the diagram shows, the **1st** card represents the primary issue involved in the question.

The **2nd** card describes your viewpoint about the situation and may show distortion or wishful thinking depending upon the card that appears here.

The **3rd** card represents the image others see of the situation in question. Since it represents the way things appear, it may or may not reflect the true state of affairs.

The **4th** card tells you what you're doing right about the issue in question.

The **5th** card shows what's missing in your perspective on the issue.

The **6th** card reveals the past that surrounds the situation. This could be recent past or even the distant past, if the person is still processing old issues related to the question.

The **7th** card is the next event or change in the situation.

The **8th** card reveals the challenge you face regarding the question.

The **9th** card tells how you can best resolve and integrate the challenge.

The **10th** card is the timing card for the events described in the spread.

The **11th** card is the best advice of the cards for now.

An Example of the Star of Insight Spread

A woman asked a question about her relationship with her boyfriend.

In position **1**, the Ace of Wands shows that there is a burst of new creative energy around the relationship.

In position **2**, the Chariot describes her viewpoint as one of motivation and confidence as she moves swiftly forward on her path. The Chariot may also describe the type of man she admires.

In position **3**, the 2 of Swords reveals that others see her in a stalemate situation with no easy resolution of difficult choices.

In position **4**, the 2 of Cups R shows that she is willing to look at areas where she and her lover differ and sometimes clash. She is allowing healthy disagreement to be expressed instead of giving in and placating her lover.

The Star of Insight Spread

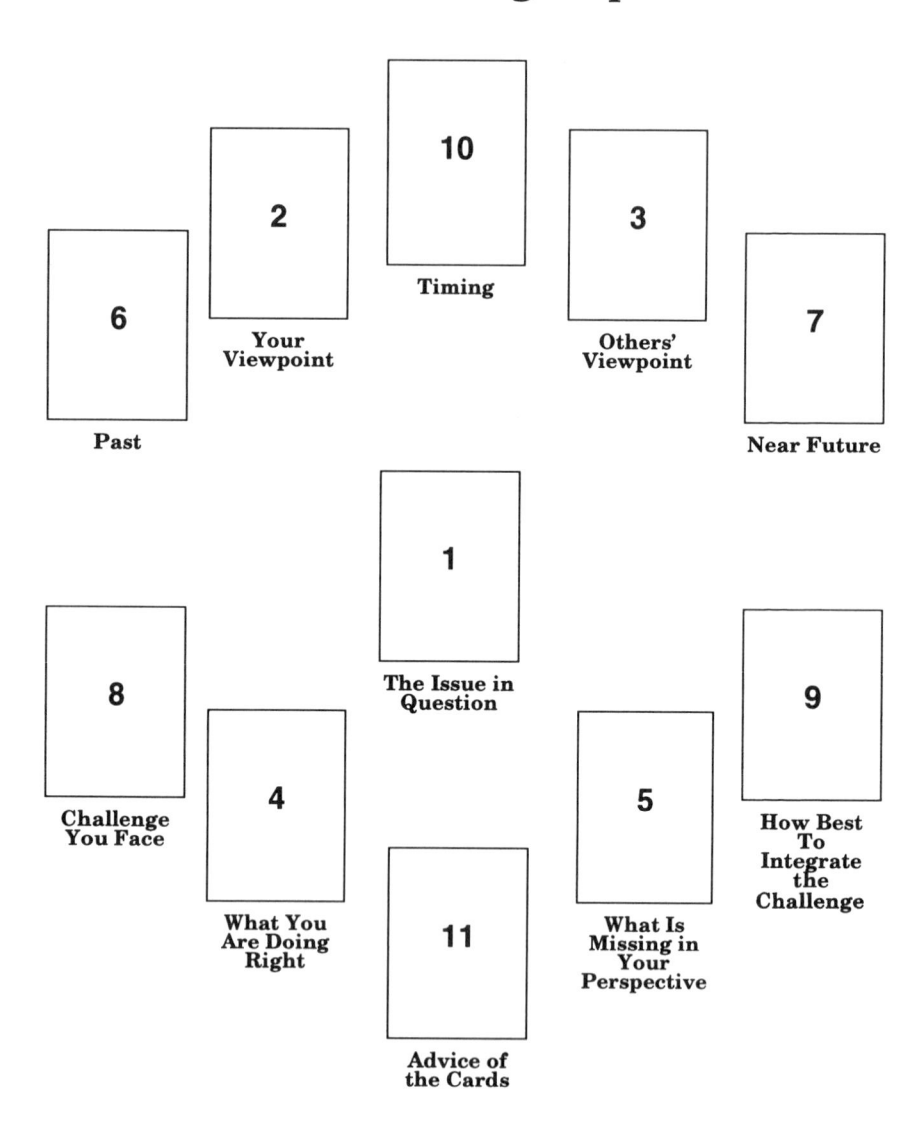

10 — Timing
2 — Your Viewpoint
3 — Others' Viewpoint
6 — Past
7 — Near Future
1 — The Issue in Question
8 — Challenge You Face
9 — How Best To Integrate the Challenge
4 — What You Are Doing Right
5 — What Is Missing in Your Perspective
11 — Advice of the Cards

In position **5**, the Star is missing in her perspective, meaning that she may not be reaching out for her ideal mate or relationship potential, thereby limiting her chances of realizing her dream.

In position **6**, the Ace of Swords shows a strong show of courage and strength in the past that has created a renewal of will in the relationship.

In position **7**, the 10 of Swords R reveals that the future of the relationship may involve painful realizations or endings, but they will not come as a surprise since the 10 of Swords is reversed.

In position **8**, the Page of Wands indicates that the challenge is to keep communication from becoming scattered, irritable, or impulsive. Repressing the creative energy promised by the Ace of Wands could also represent a challenge.

In position **9**, the King of Swords R shows the potential for either of them to behave in a calculating or manipulative way without regard for the deeper needs of the partner.

In position **10**, the 3 of Pentacles establishes the next 3 months as the timetable for the spread.

In position **11**, the Magician advises her to use her powers of intuition and manifestation of universal energy to create the magic that she desires. It implies that she may encourage her lover to express his own magical abilities.

A second layer of cards can be placed to the left of each card except cards 10 and 11 to add greater detail to each position.

The Crossroads Spread

The Crossroads Spread is a useful spread to use when confronted by a difficult decision or dilemma. It provides information about any two known options and also about a third direction that could be an unknown alternative. This third path insight can help dispel the illusion that there are only two choices available and offer some creative alternative solutions.

Meanings of Positions in the Spread

As shown in the diagram, cards **1** and **2** indicate the present influences.

Cards **3, 5,** and **7** relate to directions ahead on Path # 1.

Cards **4, 6,** and **8** refer to indications along Path # 2.

Cards **9, 11,** and **13** offer insight about Path # 3. The questioner can either identify Path # 3 before shuffling or allow this position to represent an unknown path.

Cards **10, 12,** and **14** represent advice and lessons regarding each of the three paths explored in the spread.

The **15th** card offers general advice about the best attitude or action now – in some instances indicating that the decision might be better postponed until a later time.

An additional **16th** card can be added below the 15th card to act as a timing card for the length of time that the 15th advice card would be in effect.

An Example of the Crossroads Spread

A student asked a question about whether to focus her studies on art (Path #1) or healing (Path #2).

In Position **1** and **2**, the Hermit and the King of Cups R appear indicating that she is serious about her desire for knowledge and that a kindly man over 40 is presently around her. His support for her studies is strong but he may try to do too much for her at times.

In Position **3, 5,** and **7**, the Princess of Pentacles R, Chariot, and King of Swords R show good momentum for the study of art if she overcomes her

The Crossroads Spread

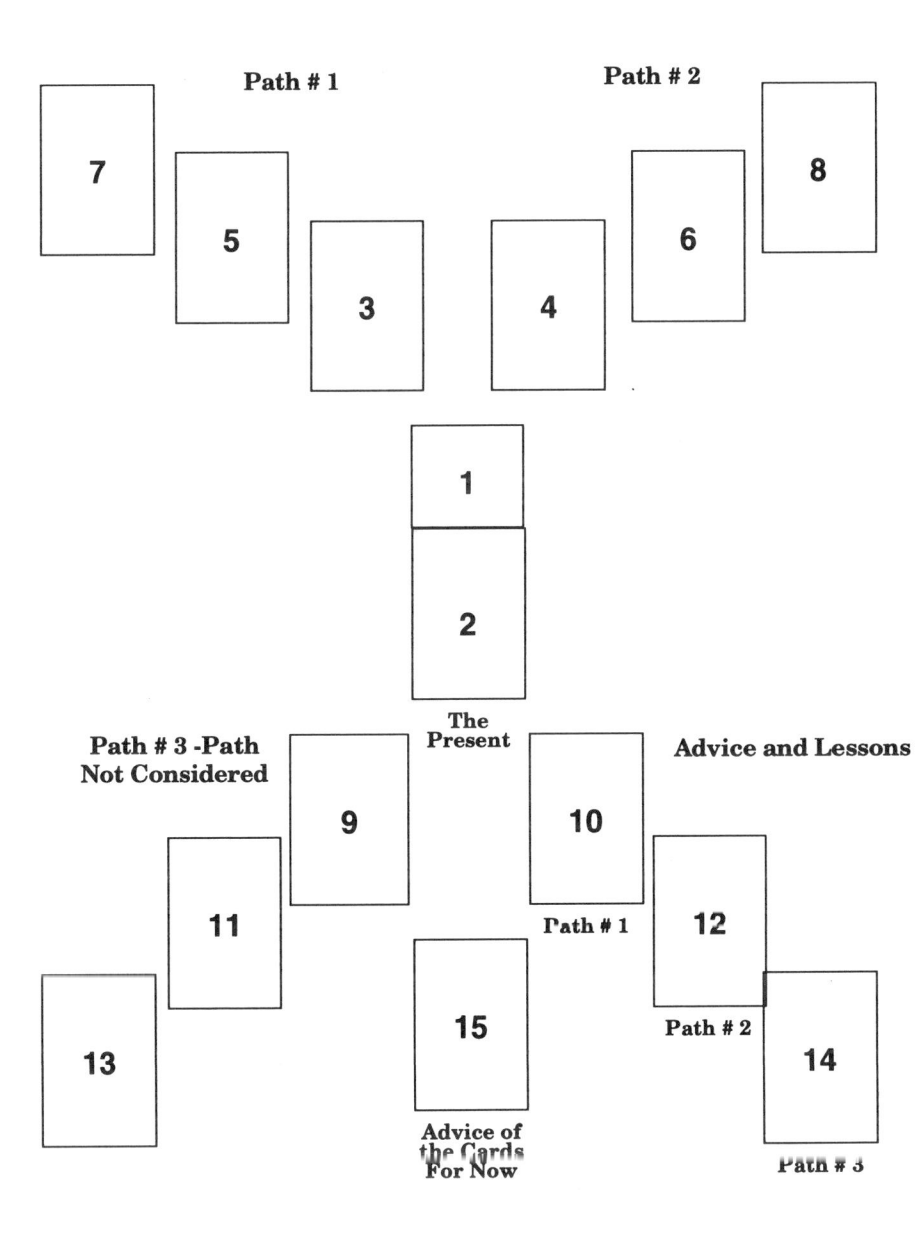

Path # 1

Path # 2

7

5

3

4

6

8

1

2

The Present

Path # 3 - Path Not Considered

Advice and Lessons

9

10

11

12

Path # 1

13

15

Path # 2

14

Advice of the Cards For Now

Path # 3

Page 133

insecurities about either her money or her scholastic abilities. The King of Swords R may represent a man over 40 who will offer intellectual stimulation but could also be demanding and abrasive. The presence of the Chariot shows high motivation and could relate to travel as part of her study and marketing of art.

In positions **4**, **6**, and **8**, Path #2 reveals the Princess of Cups R, the Hanged Man, and the 2 of Swords R. Movement in this direction could be blocked, possibly until she settles on a specific type of healing or curriculum of study. Emotional healing techniques may appeal to her with the Princess of Cups R, as well as healing of addictions with the Hanged Man present. Co-dependency therapy and love addiction healing could be areas she may wish to pursue. The 2 of Swords R shows that she will eventually clear away any ambivalence about her direction in the healing field and reach a clear decision.

In positions **9**, **11**, and **13**, we find the 10 of Cups, King of Wands R, and 9 of Swords indicating that the well-meaning goodwill of those who love her, especially the King of Wands R, could sidetrack her from her own goals and produce anxiety. The spontaneity and gambling spirit of this man over 40 can tempt her to enjoy adventures with him instead of concentrating on her goal of learning.

In positions **10**, **12**, and **14**, the advice and lessons for each of the three paths are Judgement R, the Fool R, and the 8 of Wands R respectively. Judgement R cautions her to delay before making a final decision but because it is a Major Arcana card and the Chariot refers to Path #1, this path has strong indications for positive growth. The Fool R cautions her about being naive in her pursuit of training as a healer through Path #2 and could refer to the personal healing of her inner child at this time. Personal therapy could be preferable to formal training in the healing arts. The 8 of Wands R suggests delays and hassles if she rejects both Paths # 1 and # 2 and looks in a new direction.

In position **15**, the 10 of Pentacles advises her to focus her energies at this time on enjoying financial prosperity and stable relationships in her life.

In position **16**, the 8 of Cups defines a time period of 8 days for her focus on financial, family, and business enjoyment.

In summary, the most favorable indications are for her to pursue studies and marketing products in the art field (Path #1) but only after a delay of at least eight days to concentrate on more important financial and family matters.

After the eight day time frame has expired, the Star of Insight Spread could help to further refine her direction in art.

Spreads Relating to Soul Purpose and Life Direction

The Major Arcana symbolizes the entire process of spiritual and psychological growth that we have chosen to experience in this lifetime. I see purpose not as a single fixed intention but as an evolutionary process. Our purpose shifts as we travel through the Major Arcana integrating its growth and lessons. While there are dominant themes to our lives (as when Major Arcana cards recur repeatedly), our purpose is not a static rigid goal but an ongoing unfoldment represented by the process of evolution of the Major Arcana cards.

We can repeat any of the spreads relating to purpose and life path to see our current level of awareness and integration of the lessons and experiences of previous years. For example, a person's perception of the meaning of her childhood years may reflect the pain of her alcoholic household through the 3 of Swords, the Moon, and the 8 of Swords describing her intense feeling of being confused and trapped. Later, after some recovery, the same period of her life may show the idealization of her alcoholic father with cards like the 7 of Cups, King of Cups R, and 3 of Cups R, explaining how the seeds were planted in early childhood for her future marriages to alcoholics and her own addictive behavior.

The Soul Purpose Spread

This spread uses only the Major Arcana cards and the Unknowable card to determine the purpose card in position 1.

- Spread just these cards out face down or fan them out on a table.
- Become centered in your heart center and ask for insight about your soul purpose or dominant life theme. You may want to hold a special crystal or talisman in your dominant hand (the one you write with) as you draw the cards.
- Draw three cards with your non-dominant hand, make a note of them, and return them to the cards on the table and mix them up again.
- Draw three cards as above at least three times until you have drawn the same card more than once.
- If you have more than one duplication after drawing three cards three times, place each card that was duplicated in the center of the Soul

Purpose Spread in position 1. If you draw the Unknowable card more than once, place it in the center.

- It may take more than three times to draw the same card twice – if so, keep drawing three cards until you draw a card that duplicates one you drew before. Stop after the first duplication and place that card in the center of the spread.

Meanings of Positions in the Spread

Card **1** will be either a Major Arcana card or the Unknowable and will represent your soul purpose and dominant life theme as they are expressing now.

Return all the cards to the complete deck, shuffle, and spread the cards out in the following order:

Cards **2** and **4** refer to areas where comfortable patterns need release.

Cards **3** and **5** show ways to integrate and develop new patterns.

Card **6** represents lessons and tests that will build strength and character.

Card **7** defines the advice of the cards.

Card **8** indicates areas ready for forgiveness, completion, and transformation.

Card **9** sets the timing for assimilating the next step in your personal evolution.

An Example of the Soul Purpose Spread

The questioner is a woman in her forties studying Jungian psychology.

After drawing three sets of three cards from the Major Arcana and Unknowable cards, her only duplication was the Moon card, which was placed in position **1**. The Moon card ties in closely with her interest in the archetypes of the collective unconscious and the insight that can be derived from dreams. Her development of psychic ability and intuition is highlighted at this time in her life. She could be susceptible to the doubts, paranoia, addictions, and delusions associated with this card if she loses her grounding.

Positions **2** and **4** are the Devil R and the 5 of Swords R showing her readiness to release old patterns of coping with resentment or manipulation by self-destructive measures, such as addictions. She is no longer attracted

The Soul Purpose Spread

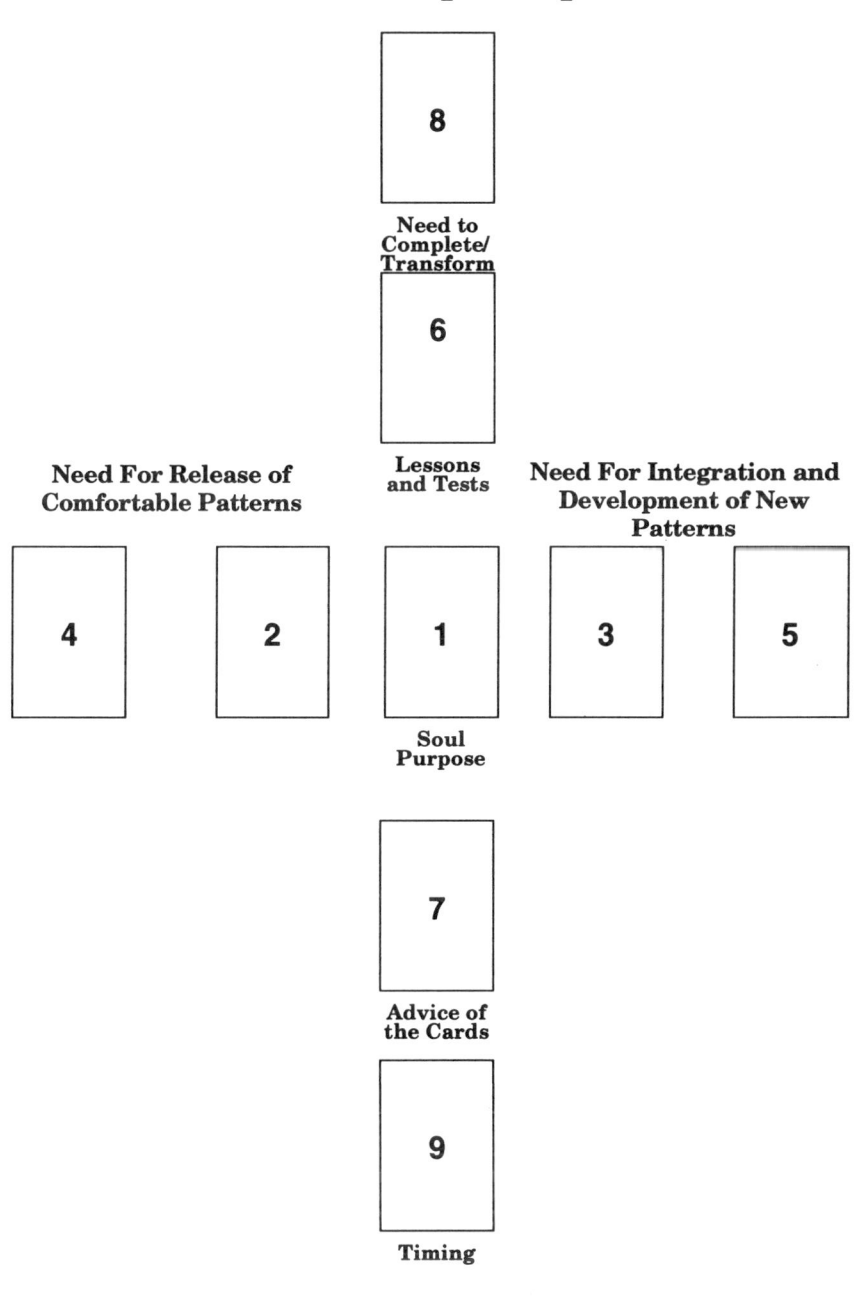

8 — Need to Complete/<u>Transform</u>

6 — Lessons and Tests

4 — Need For Release of Comfortable Patterns

2

1 — Soul Purpose

3 — Need For Integration and Development of New Patterns

5

7 — Advice of the Cards

9 — Timing

to the instant gratification of no-growth stress relief and has reached a new level of discipline and maturity.

Positions **3** and **5** reveal the High Priestess and the 7 of Wands as areas of new development and integration. She is ready to confidently maintain her intuitive perspective even when others challenge her. She can express the charisma and awareness of the High Priestess in her dealings with others as a therapist. This combination suggests the ability to stay grounded and to focus in depth on the mysteries of the unconscious.

Position **6** suggests through the 6 of Swords that she is learning to listen to good advice and to avoid choosing turbulent people and situations. There may also be tests about whether to travel or move, especially across bodies of water.

Position **7** offers advice through the 10 of Swords R about accepting the completion and release of unworkable situations in her life that are destructive or no longer appropriate.

Position **8** with the 7 of Cups R shows her completion and release of unrealistic fantasies and romantic illusions and their transformation into creative expression of her talents.

Position **9** provides timing of 5 months indicated by the 5 of Pentacles R during which the influences described in the spread can evolve.

The Life Reading Spread

The Life Reading Spread can be used to gain insight into each decade up to the present as an overview of the lessons and experiences of the past. While offering the synthesis of hindsight, it also focuses on the key issues in the present and offers advice for making wise choices in the future. The number of cards used in the spread will depend on the decade for the questioner's present age. If the questioner has just entered a new decade, by turning 40 for example, she would still place three cards in positions 16, 17, and 18. Those who are in earlier or later decades than the forties used in the diagram would add or drop three cards per decade so that the last decade shown corresponds to their age.

Meanings of Positions in the Spread

Cards **1**, **2**, and **3** refer to key issues now and the cards that appear in the other decades will reflect how those decades affected the issues at hand.

Cards **4**, **5**, and **6** symbolize the influences between ages 0-9.

Cards **7, 8,** and **9** reflect the effects of the teenage years of 10-19.

Cards **10, 11,** and **12** reveal the impact of ages 20-29.

Cards **13, 14,** and **15** show the major issues of ages 30-39.

Cards **16, 17,** and **18** relate to the influences of ages 40-49.

Card **19** refers to the advice of the cards for now.

Card **20** describes an obstacle to overcome.

Card **21** defines the timing for the present influences.

Card **22** gives clues about the next step ahead.

An Example of the Life Reading Spread

The questioner is a woman in her forties.

In positions **1, 2,** and **3**, the Tower R, 2 of Wands R, and the Prince of Pentacles suggest that the questioner is experiencing a shake-up in her life and is becoming aware of differences between her values or goals and those of the Knight of Pentacles R. This card reminded her of her brother whose earthy energy was similar to several important men in her life. She had come to a place in her evolution where she could stand up to important males in her life and express sides of her personality that might provoke disapproval from them. She agreed that the changes in her, although unsettling to her at times, were a welcome relief from her previous placating behavior.

In positions **4, 5,** and **6**, her early childhood cards were Death R, the 8 of Pentacles R, and the 7 of Swords describing severe assaults on her self-esteem, sense of competency, and trust of others with important aspects of her personality going underground at that time.

In position **7, 8,** and **9**, the Hermit, Princess of Wands R, and Queen of Wands R describe her tendency in her teen years to withdraw from others and to repress her anger and creativity. The Queen of Wands R shows her difficult relationship with her mother, who was impatient and high-strung. She learned to cope with the stress and lack of communication in her childhood environment by going inward for solace and guidance. She also spent time with her grandmother who was a mentor to her.

In position **10, 11,** and **12**, the 5 of Cups R, Queen of Cups, and 6 of Wands R show emotional disappointment and defeat during her twenties when she felt trapped in an unfulfilling marriage.

The Life Reading Spread

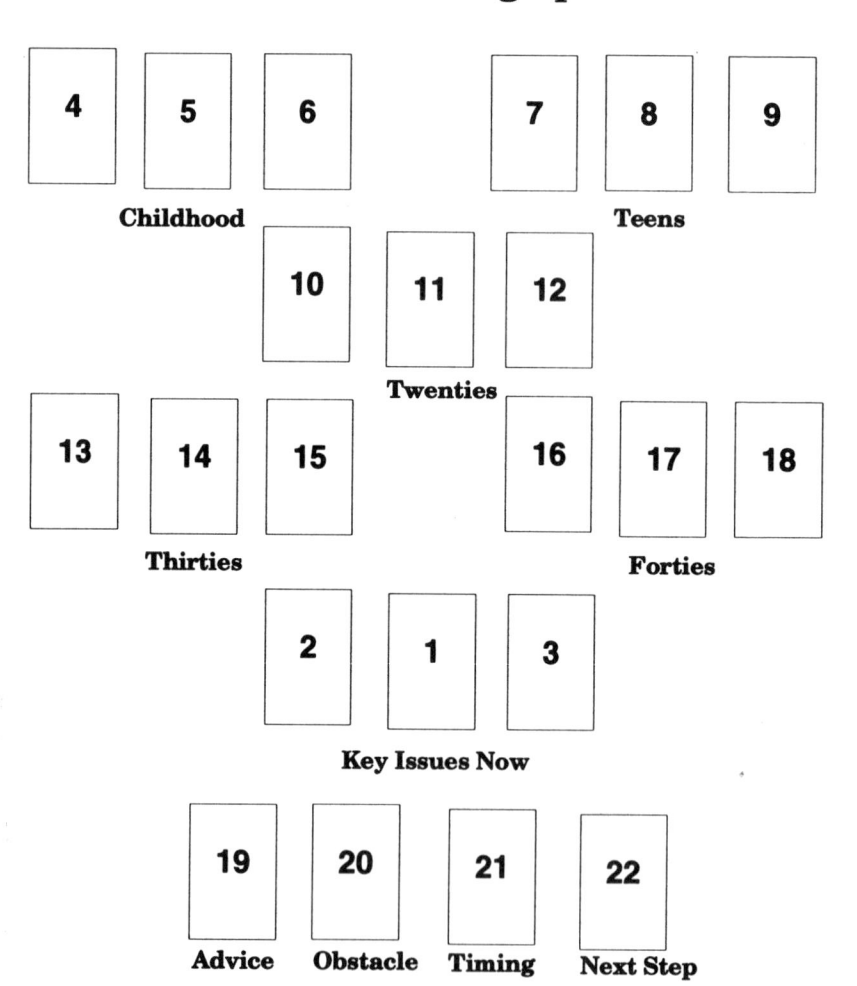

| 4 | 5 | 6 | | 7 | 8 | 9 |

Childhood   **Teens**

| 10 | 11 | 12 |

Twenties

| 13 | 14 | 15 | | 16 | 17 | 18 |

Thirties   **Forties**

| 2 | 1 | 3 |

Key Issues Now

| 19 | 20 | 21 | 22 |

Advice   **Obstacle**   **Timing**   **Next Step**

In position **13**, **14**, and **15**, the 5 of Wands, Wheel of Fortune, and 10 of Wands describe her anger at restrictive conditions, positive changes requiring risk-taking, and the heavy burdens she shouldered after her divorce. The mistrust of life and undermining of her creative expression that developed in her first two decades burst forth in her thirties with almost a reckless assertiveness that created alienation and the taking on of too many burdens for others. She was being led by fate and synchronistic events in a positive direction as she became interested in psychology and metaphysics.

In position **16**, **17**, and **18**, the Ace of Cups, 4 of Wands, and Devil R reflect her loving relationship with her partner and friends and her determination not to fall back into self-destructive patterns. The Devil R shows that the learning of lessons has created wisdom and that the old mistakes are no longer appealing.

In position **19**, the Chariot advises her to move forward on her path with momentum, confidence, and energy. Travel and exercise are beneficial.

In position **20**, the obstacle is the 3 of Cups, meaning that happy social gatherings with friends or family can be tempting and act as a distraction from the goals and direction indicated by the Chariot.

In position **21**, the 6 of Pentacles corresponds to the next 6 months as the timing for the influences described to unfold.

In position **22**, the Prince of Wands refers to the next step ahead as a change of residence or travel. The Prince of Wands can also refer to a dynamic person who may have an inspirational or adventurous impact on the questioner.

The Life Reading Update

The Life Reading Spread can be fine-tuned to give specific influences for a given day, similar to looking at the daily transits in astrology. An astrologer gives greater attention to the slower-moving influences of the outer planets because they relate to long-term processes and growth. In the same way, we can draw a card to represent a specific decade, year, month, week, and day without confusion as long as we keep in mind that the larger cycle provides the context for the smaller cycles.

- Card 1 - After you have identified your current **purpose card** (card 1) from the Soul Purpose Spread, you may want to start with that card whenever you are updating your life reading.

- Card 2 - Separate the Major Arcana cards and the Unknowable card, excluding your purpose card, and spread only those cards face down on a table. Draw one card to represent the spiritual and psychological issues for the decade you are in now. Place the **decade card** to the right of the purpose card.

- Card 3 - Without returning the purpose card or decade card to the deck, draw another card from only the Major Arcana cards and the Unknowable to represent the spiritual and psychological influences for the current year (counted from birthday to birthday). The **year card** is placed to the right of the decade card.

- Card 4 - Reassemble the entire deck, except for the purpose, decade, and year cards. Shuffle the cards well and draw a card to represent the present calendar month. You can take this card from the top, cut the cards, or spread the cards face down and select it, but the method of selection should be in your mind before you shuffle. Place the **month card** to the right of the year card.

- Card 5 - Using the same method you used to pick the month card, choose another card to represent the influences for the current week. Place the **current week card** to the right of the month card.

- Card 6 - In the same way, you can bring the update to the present day by drawing a card to represent the energies for the day. Place the **current day card** to the right of the current week card.

An Example of the Life Reading Update

The questioner is the 43 year old woman studying Jungian psychology used as the example under the Soul Purpose Spread.

In position **1**, the purpose card is the Moon card derived from the center of the Soul Purpose Spread. As described under the Soul Purpose Spread, her life direction involves exploration of the unconscious mind through archetypes, dreams, and past life memories. The development of her intuition will give her powers of discernment in times of doubt and paranoia, when she could be tempted to indulge in addictive behavior.

In position **2**, the decade card is the Tower R representing that her forties are a time of letting go of restrictions and false structures in her life. While her life could feel chaotic and unsettled at times, she has an opportunity to recreate her life from the ground up during this decade.

In position **3**, the year card is the 6 of Cups describing her 43rd year as one of reconnecting with family, friends, and positive karmic ties from past lives. She is likely to feel a strong sense of belonging and a loving acceptance from those in her environment. It is a good year for emotional sharing with kindred spirits.

The Life Reading Update

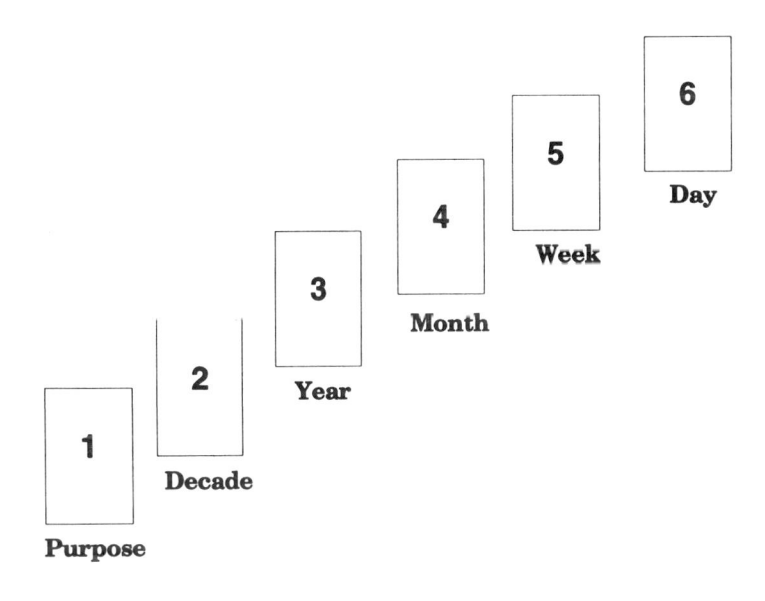

In position **4**, the month card is the Princess of Swords meaning that the current month will be a positive time for mental communication and stimulation. Writing in a clear and direct style and speaking openly about her truth are indicated. Contracts, legal matters, and gathering facts could be highlighted. A young person matching the description of the Princess of Swords could be important during this month. Since this month shows a strong energy for clarifying ideas, the nebulous aspects of the Moon card and the chaotic conditions of the Tower R card can be understood and brought into logical focus during this time period. The helpful contacts shown by the year card (6 of Cups) can provide good feedback and reliable information.

In position **5**, the week card is the Princess of Cups expressing the emotional openness and warmth to be enjoyed during this week. Social invitations, open-hearted exchanges, and loving expressions help the questioner to balance her head (Princess of Swords) with her heart. This may be a week of reconnecting with close ties. The Princess of Cups may also represent a connection with a gay person or a young emotionally sensitive person.

In position **6**, the day card is the Hierophant signifying a day for attunement to spiritual ritual or teaching, making sure that the form the ritual or instruction takes expresses its true spirit. This day could also involve dealings with conservative, rigid, or dogmatic people or institutions. This exposure will help the questioner, who is an intuitive, right-brained, liberal person to compare her mindset to others' and to keep a balanced perspective.

The Life Reading Update blends the meanings of the cards starting with the overview of long-range cards and gradually filters the information down to the more immediate and specific level. In this way, the focus on both overall life purpose and immediate everyday experience can be maintained. It is often helpful to leave this spread out on an altar or nightstand as a reminder of the key focus areas.